Cambridge El

Elements in American Politics
edited by
Frances E. Lee
Princeton University

THE DYNAMICS OF PUBLIC OPINION

Mary Layton Atkinson
University of North Carolina, Charlotte

K. Elizabeth Coggins
Colorado College

James A. Stimson
University of North Carolina, Chapel Hill

Frank R. Baumgartner
University of North Carolina, Chapel Hill

CAMBRIDGE
UNIVERSITY PRESS

University Printing House, Cambridge CB2 8BS, United Kingdom

One Liberty Plaza, 20th Floor, New York, NY 10006, USA

477 Williamstown Road, Port Melbourne, VIC 3207, Australia

314–321, 3rd Floor, Plot 3, Splendor Forum, Jasola District Centre,
New Delhi – 110025, India

103 Penang Road, #05–06/07, Visioncrest Commercial, Singapore 238467

Cambridge University Press is part of the University of Cambridge.

It furthers the University's mission by disseminating knowledge in the pursuit of
education, learning, and research at the highest international levels of excellence.

www.cambridge.org
Information on this title: www.cambridge.org/9781009100595
DOI: 10.1017/9781108871266

Mary Layton Atkinson, K. Elizabeth Coggins, James A. Stimson, and
Frank R. Baumgartner 2021

First published 2021

A catalogue record for this publication is available from the British Library.

ISBN 978-1-009-10059-5 Hardback
ISBN 978-1-108-81911-4 Paperback
ISSN 2515-1606 (online)
ISSN 2515-1592 (print)

The Dynamics of Public Opinion

Elements in American Politics

DOI: 10.1017/9781108871266
First published online: September 2021

Mary Layton Atkinson
University of North Carolina, Charlotte

K. Elizabeth Coggins
Colorado College

James A. Stimson
University of North Carolina, Chapel Hill

Frank R. Baumgartner
University of North Carolina, Chapel Hill

Author for correspondence: James A. Stimson, jstimson@email.unc.edu

Abstract: A central question in political representation is whether government responds to the people. To understand that, we need to know what the government is doing, and what the people think of it. We seek to understand a key question necessary to answer those bigger questions: How does American public opinion move over time? We posit three patterns of change over time in public opinion, depending on the type of issue. Issues on which the two parties (Democratic and Republican) regularly disagree provide clear partisan cues to the public. For these party cue issues we present a slight variation on the thermostatic theory from Soroka and Wlezien (2010) and Wlezien (1995); our "implied thermostatic model." A smaller number of issues divide the public along lines unrelated to partisanship, and so partisan control of government provides no relevant clue. Finally, we note a small but important class of issues which capture response to cultural shifts.

Keywords: opinion, policy, mood, agendas, thermostat, cycles
JEL classifications: A12, B34, C56, D78, E90

ISBNs: 9781009100595 (HB), 9781108819114 (PB), 9781108871266 (OC)
ISSNs: 2515-1606 (online), 2515-1592 (print)

Contents

1 Introduction

Begin with our title, "Dynamics of Public Opinion." Why opinion dynamics? Why do we care how public sentiment moves over time? We could care about opinions for the same sort of reasons that collectors care about coins or stamps, just for the joy of collecting. But we do not collect just because we like collecting. (And, in fact, collecting data from thousands of surveys as we have done here does not necessarily spark joy; it is not satisfying on its own.) We care about opinion dynamics because theory – democratic theory – requires that we do. Democratic theory mandates a system in which policy-making responds to public demands. And we cannot understand the black box that is politics unless we understand public demands.

In this Element we aim to get inside that box, called representation, to gain purchase on American politics by coming to understand how opinion moves. That is our goal. We are ambitious. We wish to understand *all* of what Americans want from government, spanning multiple dimensions. We will propose that three models – only three – are needed to understand virtually all opinion movement in American politics. Jointly the three models form a theory of opinion movement. We will observe that public opinion sometimes cycles over time, sometimes trends in one direction, and sometimes (rarely) does not move at all. Our definition of success in this endeavor will require us to take everything we know about politics, and how political parties compete over policy-making and elections, to explain the variations in opinion movement. To the extent that we succeed in these pages, the reader will come to think that the whole system we propose could not be otherwise. But of course success in scholarship is halting and partial. Readers perhaps will be unconvinced.

The study of representation hinges on accurately measuring public preferences for government services, and assessing the relationship between those demands and government outputs. This Element makes advances in both areas. First, we develop a theory that outlines the important role political parties play in facilitating public responsiveness to government action. On issues where the parties regularly take opposing positions (most welfare state policies for example), the public can infer the direction of policy change in Washington simply by knowing which party is in control of the White House. Opinion, therefore, cycles over time in response to changes in party control. In fact, this is the single most prominent mechanism of opinion change, explaining the majority of the cases we will analyze in the pages to come. But, as good as it is, the party-based model is an incomplete one; there are two others. Where party cues are absent, or where cleavages other than partisanship are dominant, different patterns of public response emerge.

One understudied and generally poorly understood area of opinion change relates to those areas where the political parties do not take opposing positions. On some issues, nearly all Americans agree, or their disagreements relate to things other than their party preferences, ideological positions, or other factors connected to elections and voting. Political scientists (and public opinion polling firms) typically pay little attention to these areas of public policy, since by definition they are aside from the stuff of politics; they will not affect any election outcomes. If these issues don't regularly divide the major parties and don't align with the ideological divides that separate us, these issues cannot logically affect electoral outcomes. But they still exist; people still have those attitudes, and we should understand them. We make some initial steps toward doing so here. They may cycle, or remain relatively stable over time, but they cannot cycle in the same way that partisan issues cycle. This is because the main driver of change for partisan issues – citizen response to the inferred direction of policy change based on control of the White House – is impossible. If the parties don't differ in their positions on these issues, then the public cannot infer anything related to them on the basis of which party controls the government. So we will develop one model for issues that regularly divide the parties, one for those that don't, and a third, which follows.

Our third and last model of attitude change over time relates to issues that concern long-term cultural shifts. These are social transformations affecting society in powerful ways, literally shifting the norms of cultural acceptability of a given issue position. These can be so powerful that they overwhelm the influence of any short-term partisan differences, driving substantial shifts in public opinion over time, all in the same direction. We use the examples of racial attitudes, attitudes toward women's equality, and attitudes toward the rights of gay Americans to illustrate this third pattern of change. Change in these "cultural shift" policy domains is steady over the long term. The influence of short term partisan differences on these issues is overwhelmed by the longer-term trends associated with two factors: (1) large swaths of the American public progressively adopting new, pro-equality positions on the issue, and (2) the generational replacement of individuals with once-widespread but no-longer-majority anti-equality opinions with younger individuals coming of age during a different time, and reflecting more progressive positions on these cultural shift issues.

The first two models of opinion dynamics we identify imply no long-term change in opinion at all. In these cases, aggregate opinion moves up and down (or, left and right) but fifty years later remains roughly where it started. Cycles and movements occur, but these are centered around some mean opinion, and this mean opinion shows relative stability when considered over a long period of time. The third model is not like that at all. Absolute change associated with issues of cultural shift reflects shifting societal values and results in long-term opinion trends.

Our simple proposal is that there are three, and only three, models needed to understand opinion dynamics. These relate to three types of issues: partisan, nonpartisan, and cultural shift. Partisan issues cover the bulk of public opinion questions of interest to most political scientists, and most often posed by commercial and academic polling organizations. These correspond to what has been called the "thermostatic" model of opinion change (Soroka and Wlezien 2010; Wlezien 1995). Nonpartisan issues will fail any statistical test for thermostatic response to change in party control of government because the key driver there is missing: there is no difference in expected policy outcomes on these issues based on who is in control. Both parties support the maintenance of our national parks, for example; we cannot infer a position on the space program based on which party is in power. So, if opinion to these policies remains stable, drifts, or cycles, it will do so out of sync with partisan issues. Finally, for cultural shift issues, trends will occur. Absolute opinion change, combined with generational replacement, facilitates long-term absolute shifts in aggregate public opinion. These are so powerful that they overwhelm any short-term partisan differences that may surface. No political party can ignore these trends for long and remain in power – public policies change dramatically over time in response to shifting cultural values, which in turn reinforces the opinion trends.

Our starting point for the theoretical framework we develop is the well-known thermostatic model. We support this model and believe it is simple, accurate, and useful. We build on it by outlining the key role of consistent party cues in shaping citizen inferences. Consistent party cues allow citizens to draw inferences about the direction of public policy simply by knowing which party controls the levers of government. The simplicity of this model is one of its merits, and it also defines the limits of its applicability: to all issues where the parties regularly take opposing sides. That is, logically the model should hold only when such cues are present. Where consistent party cues are not present, the model cannot hold. And, where cultural shifts are so powerful as to overwhelm partisan differences, the model cannot hold. So, we start with the thermostatic model and add two adjustments. The resulting tri-fold model of opinion change incorporates the original model but completes it with two additional models relevant to different types of issues.

None of what we write here should diminish the power of the thermostatic model. In fact, because most policy issues are consistently politicized – and because we show that very low levels of public knowledge about government are needed for the thermostat to work – the model applies to the vast majority of cases. But there are topics on which the parties do not regularly take opposing views. On issues like funding for NASA, social security and drug treatment programs, the parties typically agree. Policy outputs in these domains remain consistent over time, even when party control in Washington changes. As a result, public opinion on these topics does not respond to partisan control of government.

Still other issues, like civil rights for racial minorities, women and members of the LGBTQ community, activate cleavages that transcend the partisan divide. Here, social movements have challenged societal norms and promoted the expansion of rights for groups that historically have been marginalized. As individuals embrace these new, inclusive values, demand for government policies that facilitate equality increases. This represents absolute rather than relative opinion change. Public opinion on these issues trends over time rather than cycling in response to changes in party control. These trends are due, in large part, to generational replacement. Individuals from younger cohorts are socialized in a more inclusive environment, leading them to more fully embrace pro-rights values than did members of older cohorts. As public opinion moves in a liberal, pro-equality direction over time, so too, does public policy. And, as we have mentioned, some cultural shifts are so great that, over two decades or more, they bring us to places not previously imagined or taken seriously, such as the legalization of gay marriage.

We begin with the reigning model of the process, the "thermostatic" model of Wlezien and Soroka (Soroka and Wlezien 2010; Wlezien 1995). The thermostatic model uses the metaphor of the home thermostat to explain how citizens regulate policy-making. Its essence is that citizens have a preference for comfortable temperatures. And so when the house strays in one direction or the other from that ideal they can regulate the system simply by turning the thermostat up or down. Note how undemanding the thermostat is. People need not understand the physics of home heating and need not even know the current inside temperature. All they need to know is "too hot" or "too cold" and the corrective action is obvious. Similarly when policy-making is too liberal or too conservative (or perceived to be) they can call for it to reverse to get back to the citizen's ideal. The general prediction that emerges from this process is that the direction of opinion change is opposite to the dominant direction of change in policy. Liberal policy produces a conservative reaction and conservative policy produces a liberal reaction.

Although we will offer small modifications to the model, we regard it as spectacularly successful. So our critiques to come should be seen as small modifications to a theory we admire. It could not be as successful as it is if it were far wrong.

1.1 The Thermostat and the Implied Thermostat

The thermostatic model of Wlezien (1995) assumes that citizens react to actual policy making. Citizens compare their personal preferences for the level of policy to what government is doing currently and react in the opposite direction if policy is tending too far left or right of their personal ideal point. This model has one very big virtue: it works. Knowing the direction that policy is tending, one can predict that opinion will tend in the opposite direction and be right a good proportion of the time.

But it is a bit strange that the thermostatic model works – and, indeed, works well. What is strange is that the assumption that citizens are knowledgeable of current policy-making is strikingly contrary to most public opinion scholarship. The dominant view of political science is that citizens are normally inattentive, with public affairs well down the list of things they care about, and well down the list of things to which they assign their precious time. Since knowing the current direction of policy is intellectually demanding, it seems unlikely that it could be true that citizens track policy direction for more than the most publicized issues of the moment. When the George W. Bush Administration slashed taxes in 2001 and again in 2003, the public was probably aware that tax policy was moving in the conservative direction. But policy is moving in dozens of domains (many of which we will quantify) and most of these, most of the time, are invisible to all but the hyper attentive.

So how can it be that a theory successfully predicts opinion movement when its central underlying assumption is dubious? Posing that question leads us to postulate a supplemental, and simplifying, mechanism that facilitates knowledge of policy change. We begin an answer by assuming that the mass public in the aggregate knows two facts about American politics. The first is that the Democrats are the party of expanding government liberalism, the party that does more, spends more, and taxes more, while Republicans are and do the opposite.[1] Not everybody knows this, as we have known at least since Campbell (1960), but it is known in the aggregate. Secondly, almost everybody knows who the current president is and which party he or she represents. Knowing those two facts permits an *inference* about the current direction of policy change. If a Democrat occupies the White House, policy is probably changing (in all domains) in a liberal direction. If a Republican is in office, policy change will be toward conservatism. This inference will usually be correct.

---

[1] Except in the instance of national defense, where Republicans do more and spend more vis-á-vis Democrats.

1.1.1 Party Control and Public Inference

Although short on political knowledge of specific kinds, the electorate does know which party controls the White House at any given time. We postulate that it uses this knowledge to make inferences about public policy. If, for example, Democrats are in power, regardless of the specifics of legislation proposed or acted upon, the public infers that policy is changing in a liberal, government expanding, direction. This is a critical shortcut that reaches essentially similar conclusions about what government is doing (and spending) to what would emerge from detailed and careful knowledge, but obviates the need for attention to details. How would we explain, for example, that Barack Obama's Affordable Care Act was perceived as a decisively liberal approach to heath care, when its central feature, the individual mandate, was a product of the conservative Heritage Foundation and the whole plan, based on private sector providers and insurers, emulated the program put forward by Mitt Romney, a Republican, in Massachusetts? The answer is inference. The plan was crafted by President Obama's congressional allies, championed by him, and passed almost entirely by Democratic votes. Therefore, it was liberal by inference.[2]

In contrast to Soroka and Wlezien (2010), we do not posit that the electorate knows – or needs to know – things like the general level of appropriations. That is a lot of detail and complexity. One can just infer that spending is probably up if Democrats are in the White House or down if Republicans are in control.[3] Crucially that means that all that needs to be known with any certainty is which party is in power. The rest can be inferred, with a decent, if imperfect, level of accuracy. Thus we propose opinion that behaves thermostatically, becoming more conservative when liberals are in power and more liberal when conservatives are in power. Therefore our modification of the Wlezien (1995) and Soroka and Wlezien (2010) theory is this: we posit that citizens either know the direction of policy change (probably not very often) or infer it from knowing who occupies the White House and the policy brand of that party (much more often). Since the inference is usually correct, the connection between known or inferred policy change and opinion outcome is robust. This we call the *implied*

---

[2] This inference was made stronger still by the policy's popular moniker, "Obamacare." Congressional Republicans, who popularized the label, understood very clearly that linking the policy to the Democratic president would increase public perception that the plan was a liberal one.

[3] Is it safe to assume that citizens know which party advocates more spending? It is. For this point data are available. The question has been posed pretty directly in American National Election Studies (ANES) surveys since the 1970s. To cite one example, in the most recent study the modal response on the ANES spending and services tradeoff scale is the most extreme spending category (1) for the Democratic candidate (Biden) and the most extreme "fewer services" category (7) for the Republican candidate (Trump). The scale means are 5.32 (Democratic) and 2.84 (Republican), where 4 is neutral.

thermostatic model. With this, we hope to distinguish our revised model from the original. It amounts to the idea that citizens respond to changes in partisan control of the White House. It is clear that we are pushing the limits of simplicity here to their maximum.

Our preference for simplicity and theoretical clarity is so strong that we also do not incorporate divided versus unified government into our theory, though doing so could be a useful exercise in the future. Clearly, our theory applies most strongly during periods of unified government. In this situation, the public can most confidently infer that one party is in control. And of course, to the extent that congressional majorities are greater, this would be even more strongly the case. In periods of divided control, members of the public may be subjected to mixed messages about who really is "in control" of the government. Still, we expect members of the public to respond to White House control, not control of the House or the Senate. President Trump faced a Democratic House of Representatives during his last two years in office, but the public responded to Trump, not House Speaker Nancy Pelosi in assessing the direction in which the government in Washington was headed. The signal under unified government should be stronger than that under divided government, but even under divided government we expect the public to respond to White House control. Under divided government, it is clear that signals would not be as strong and therefore the thermostatic response might be expected to be weaker. If we were to limit the tests that we conduct in the pages below only to periods of unified government, we would expect them to be even stronger than we show. If we find support in the pages to come for our simple theory, as we do, then a slightly more complicated theory incorporating divided versus unified government, might find even stronger support. But our theoretical interest is not in divided government, so we do not focus on this question. Rather, we want to distinguish among three types of issues, only one of which is subjected to the thermostatic response.

1.1.2 Giving Credit Where It Is Due

We did not develop or name the thermostatic model. Wlezien did that. And Soroka and Wlezien refined it. And yet the empirical test we will propose for our version of the model is not the original; indeed we are simplifying in a way that the original developers of the thermostat did not, and we doubt that they made their decisions lightly. To differentiate our simplified model from the the original Wlezien "thermostatic model," we call it the *implied* thermostatic model. Our implied thermostatic model applies widely; in fact it explains the bulk of the opinion series we analyze in the pages to come. But its scope is not universal.

We can now state the limits of the implied thermostat. It works where party cues are regular and powerful, in cases of issue conflict. On issues where the party positions are mixed, confused, or episodic, it does not work. The public cannot infer party positions where the parties do not regularly take opposing positions. There are many issues where the parties take no stand at all. And there are many where the stands require more knowledge of the history of policy disputes than the mass public possesses. Where knowing party positions is easy, the thermostat dominates. Where it is not easy, the thermostat fails.

Our micro theory implies a model of macro-level opinion dynamics. We take that up now.

1.2 Three Kinds of Issues

Begin with partisan issues. These are the main line of party disagreement resulting from The New Deal and Great Society programs, issues about the role of government in the economy, regulation, the social safety net and, in general, the scope of government (how much it should do, how much it should spend, and how much it should tax to pay for that spending). The Democrats regularly take the liberal, government expanding, position. The Republicans regularly take the conservative, government contracting, position. This description fits the general tendency, but the scope of these conflicts has an elastic boundary and changes over time.

Because these sorts of issues are of central importance for party and ideological controversy, they are well and frequently measured in survey research. Opinion surveys tend to measure that which is interesting, and being at the center of party politics makes these issues interesting. Although we have no theory of the potential issue space, we can imagine that it could be vastly larger than these party conflict issues, but with large numbers of *potential* issues lacking the interest that would make them subject to survey questions.

Not every public issue leads to party conflict. Among the policy choices that government must attend to, there are many that may never become party-defining issues. The Federal Government regularly makes decisions about what to do in space travel, how much to fund science, how to regulate public lands, and what rules should govern national parks. In these and many other issue areas the conflicts about what to do have not typically broken along party lines.[4] As a consequence the distinctive party cues that the thermostatic model requires

---

[4] Certainly, there have been brief periods when many of these issues have become politicized at the national level; that is, we might say they have been "episodically" partisan. Recent debates over opening federal land to drilling, for instance, have politicized some aspects of public land management. But in the larger scheme of things – over the span of forty, fifty, or sixty years – policymaking in these areas has not typically been the subject of partisan debate.

do not exist. Democratic and Republican governments make pretty much the same decisions in these areas. Surely there are genuine conflicts in each of these cases. But they are not *party* conflicts. The thermostatic model is not false for these cases. It simply doesn't apply.

Most opinion change in the thermostatic account is relative change. Citizens with relatively fixed views encounter the changing stimulus of the parties alternating in power, and adjust their views accordingly. Liberal party cues make the electorate more conservative and conservative party cues make it more liberal. And this could be true even if no citizen ever changed views in an absolute sense.

The thermostatic model, both in its original formulation and in our slightly altered "implied" version, explains *relative* change in public opinion. Citizens come to support *more* or *less* government *relative* to the level of (perceived) current policy. They could do so with perfectly fixed opinions because the causal force of the model is change in government policy. A citizen who supports level x of policy can rationally call for more or less government policy if the government is currently pursuing more than x or less than x.

But we can imagine what we shall call absolute opinion change as yet a third possibility. In this view, citizens may change their policy preferences relative to their previous preferences, becoming more liberal or conservative on some issue, for example. And the distinctive difference of such absolute opinion change is that it does not depend upon party cues. If something happens that leads people to change their views, some real response to a real stimulus (e.g., war, depression, social movement), then that change will tend to be permanent and it will not be responsive to party cues. And contrary to Soroka and Wlezien's contention, these changes can occur in domains of true public importance. Because we do not posit the party cue as the cause of the change, there is equally no reason to expect a reversal when there is a change of party control.[5]

On this set of potential issues the implied thermostatic model is the wrong model. It posits changing party cues (from changing party control) as the causal force, and for these hypothetical cases (which we will see are real cases) that is simply the wrong causal model. Something else is causing opinion change and it does not cease or alter with a change of party control.

Our theory of the role of party cues thus borrows from the thermostatic account for the important set of issues where the parties regularly offer up

---

[5] There is a partially related distinction between absolute and relative in the format of survey questions. Sometimes they ask the absolute in the form "What should government do?" and sometimes they ask the relative, "Should government do more or less than it is currently doing?"

opposite cues. But it also needs to explain opinion dynamics in cases where the party cues do not particularly matter. Thus, party cues play one leading role in our theory of what drives opinion change in the American context.

Of our distinction of issue types, here we deal with the crucially important difference between absolute and relative (i.e., thermostatic) change. We expand this theory of opinion change to include the stimuli of generational changes, our second leading actor. We posit that those stimuli – whether they be the reframing of an issue by a successful social movement, or a set of powerful, connected events – are the force that induces real opinion change among individuals *and* generational change. These stimuli induce absolute opinion change.

1.2.1 Absolute and Thermostatic Opinion Change

Public opinion is in part response to the stimulus of government action. Thus, it may be interpreted as the answer to the question, "What does the public want from government?" Or, since government action changes over time, it may be a relative response to what government has done recently. If policy were as simple as how much to spend, for example, the first type of opinion – which we will call "absolute" – would be the dollar figure for a particular program. The second type – "relative" or thermostatic – would express a desire for more or less spending than the current level.

Relative attitudes might change either because (a) an individual alters his or her absolute preferences, or (b) an individual with fixed preferences encounters changing government policy and thus alters back and forth between more and less to maintain a fixed position in light of a changing government. While empirically separating absolute and relative changes is a challenging task, we would like here to separate them into ideal types to clarify their theoretical standing.

1.2.2 Relative Preference Change

For theoretical clarity, assume that people have fixed (absolute) preferences over policy options. Assume also that government policy changes with changes in party control of the White House. Thus a rational public will change relative attitudes to accommodate changed policy with its position.

How does this micro theory of the loosely informed citizen responding to changing party cues and control of government yield predictions about the shape of aggregate public opinion? That is our task now, turning theory into model.

1.3 A Model of Aggregate Dynamics

Here we wish to introduce some assumptions about the electorate and deduce the result of them. First, instead of a single individual, we will assume an electorate which is distributed over a scale of absolute preferences from left to right. Then we will expose this electorate to changing government policy over time.

Assume, for the sake of argument, that each member of our hypothetical electorate has absolutely fixed preferences. Assume also cardinal utility on a scale from 0 to 100. Assume two parties, D and R, with mean policy positions left and right of the median voter. For a specific illustration – but the logic is more general – we will place the parties at 30 (D) and 70 (R).

Assume that we measure relative attitudes with a question of the form, "Should government do more, less, or about the same as it is currently doing?" What are the induced dynamics?

If we divide the population into three groups, it is possible to deduce the response. Consider three groups as follows:

- **Group A**: All of those people with preferences less than or equal to D (i.e., to the left of 30).
- **Group B**: All of those people situated between D and R (30 and 70, i.e., moderates).
- **Group C**: All of those people with preferences greater than or equal to R (i.e., to the right of 70).

Now we ask how will the three groups respond to a change of party control – say from D to R? The year 2017, the shift from Obama to Trump, is an example case. That will induce a typical policy change from D's normal policy around 30 to R's normal policy around 70. See Figure 1 for an illustration of the hypothetical response.

- **Group A**: Prefers policies to the left of D and will not be affected by the change. It will assert, as it had before the change, that government should do more. Bars are black.
- **Group B**: Preferred "less" on balance (because the D government was to its left) and will now shift to "more" on balance (because the new R government is to its right). Bars are black.
- **Group C**: Prefers policies to the right of R and will not be affected by the change. It will assert "less" as it did before the change. Bars are white.

Notice that everyone under these assumptions either stays constant (A and C) or shifts from "less" to "more" (B). Thus the net shift for the electorate as a whole is from less to more, the expected thermostatic response. Thus with no

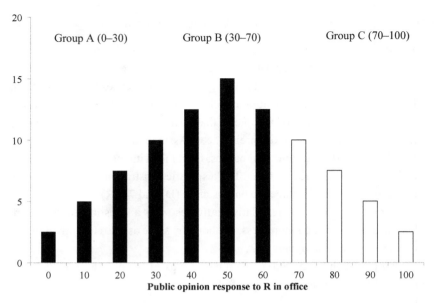

Figure 1 Public opinion response to party R in control of the White House: black bars show demands for more government; white bars show demand for less

actual change of preferences we get a relative change in preferences because the stimulus alters with party control of the presidency. Note also that in this hypothetical scenario, all categories observe the party in power and infer the same policy position for it. In the real world things would be more complicated, but this simplification captures the essential dynamic.

In Figure 2 we illustrate the reverse scenario, the shift of control from R to D. The year 2009, the shift from Bush to Obama, is an example case.

What about a neutral case? We have none because the White House is always occupied by either D or R. The electorate is exposed to too much government (D) or too little government (R), but never just right.

1.3.1 Calibrating Dynamics

With these simple assumptions, our little model does not yield any predictions about the level of our preference concept, just that it changes as a result of party change and that the direction of change will always be opposite to the position of the party of the president. For the sake of simplicity let us now assume away indifference. That is, we will not allow any of our hypothetical citizens to think that the level of current policy is about right. Instead we will force them to choose between "do more" and "do less." We will also need to assume that the numbers of the three types are equal. With these

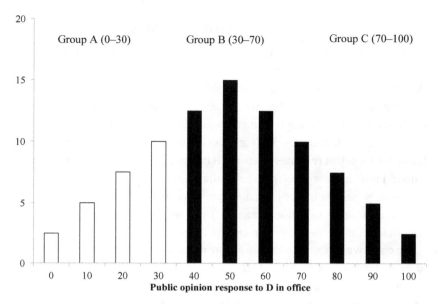

Figure 2 Public opinion response to party D in control of the White House: black bars show demands for more government; white bars show demand for less

admittedly unrealistic assumptions we can predict what our expressed preferences would be.

Now we introduce a hypothetical measure of preferences, the percent of the public advocating more government. Our hypothetical measure will be the percent of those saying that government should do more divided by the totals for "do more" and "do less." This is liberalism as understood in the American context. Thus for the initial period when government is controlled by D, group A will say that government should do more and B and C will say it should do less, a score of 33.3 because one third are asserting "do more." After the transition to party R, A and B will join together in asserting "do more," producing a score of 66.7. A further transition back to D will similarly produce a score of 33.3. And so forth.

If we now assume regular changes of party control and policy – every eight to twelve years – then the relative public opinion response will cycle over that same period. If this implied thermostatic model is correct, and we hold to our assumption that absolute preferences are fixed, then the mean of aggregate public opinion will tend to cycle left and right opposite changes in party control of the White House over time. And indeed it does, as many scholars have shown (Erikson, MacKuen, and Stimson 2002; Merrill, Grofman, and Brunell 2008; Soroka and Wlezien 2010; Stimson 1999).

1.3.2 Absolute Preference Change

What of absolute preference changes where the individual is changing from a previous level of preference for some policy to a different one? Perhaps he or she thinks at one time that gays and lesbians should be subject to discrimination and later decides that they should not be. Absolute changes would not be explained by changes in government policy. Some other stimulus is required. Whatever that stimulus may be (e.g., successful social movements or a powerful social event that reframes an issue), it induces both absolute opinion change among individuals and sets the ball rolling for generational change. We are deliberately general in our language here – we aim to put forth the theory of what causes absolute opinion change. Thus, we make room for a variety of stimuli to set this type of opinion change in motion.

We conceive of absolute change as true opinion change, either by individuals or by generations or by both. If true change is occurring, then it will *not* be subjected to cancellation or reversal by changed government policy. Absolute change is not a response to a cycling stimulus and therefore there is no reason to expect it to cycle.

1.3.3 Constant Preferences

Another logical possibility is no change at all. In the absence of partisan differences or differences in attitudes based on birth cohort, some opinion series may be stable over time. (These may also not regularly be surveyed, as they are not politicized and are rarely a topic of public debate – so we may not see much written about them in the public opinion literature, and indeed there may be little documentation about them at all.) Such topics include, for example, the management of national parks and policies related to NASA.[6]

In order to test this theory, we need to do two things. First, we need to develop the data. And second, we need to provide a test for whether, in fact, opinion change is thermostatic. Before putting the theory of party cues to the test, we pause to lay out the development of our dataset, large numbers of opinion time series.

---

[6] Attitudes toward abortion provide a rare example of an issue that has been highly politicized (since *Roe* v. *Wade*) and yet receives nearly constant levels of public support and opposition over time. Attitudes on this topic may exhibit stability despite the politicized nature of the issue because the federal government rarely changes federal policies on the issue (though politicians may discuss it frequently), providing little stimulus for public reaction.

1.4 Developing Policy Specific Moods

To test our theory, we develop and classify more than sixty new measures of policy specific mood.[7] Each of these time series measures captures macro-level demand for government liberalism in policy domains ranging from taxes, to health care reform, to air pollution, to women's rights. For the first time, we are able to study the dynamics of public opinion on a broad array of specific policy topics over the course of decades. For each topic, we assess the degree to which the issue has been consistently politicized, and test whether public opinion cycles, trends, or remains flat over time. We then take a close look at the types of policies that fit each model of opinion dynamics, and further explore the relationships between policy outputs and public preferences that define them.

To create the policy-specific public mood database, we began with Stimson's (1991) policy mood database: a rich collection of repeated survey questions asked to the public over the past seventy years.[8] Stimson's original purpose was to develop a global level measure of domestic policy mood: a single time-serial estimate of the public's changing views. To do so, Stimson collected all available survey questions that tapped into public policy preferences, ranging from matters of education, to the environment, to business regulation, to minority aid – and everything else in the domestic policy domain.[9] Using the dyad ratios algorithm, Stimson estimated a single longitudinal measure that encapsulated the public's desire for more or less government.

Scholars across subfields embraced the measurement of global policy mood. For the first time, there existed a comprehensive, robust, and longitudinal reading of the public's disposition. Scholars studying public attitudes toward particular policy topics, such as aid to minorities, welfare, abortion, and so on, have long been interested in creating similar measures for their specific areas of interest.[10] In most instances, the data were not "thick" enough to permit this

---

[7] This project was supported by NSF grant 1024291 for "Developing Policy-Specific Measures of Public Opinion," James A. Stimson and Frank R. Baumgartner, co-principal investigators.

[8] Estimated series are available at www.comparativeagendas.net/. Users are also able to create their own series, selecting specific survey questions to build unique series in real time as well as utilize our pre-estimated series based on the Policy Agendas coding scheme. To see all the documentation for the series used in this book, and the data please see our dedicated book website at http://fbaum.unc.edu/books/Opinion/Opinion.htm Note that the data we use in this book are a subset consisting of only those twenty-seven series with forty or more years of coverage, but more data is available on the Comparative Agendas Project website.

[9] For a detailed account of criteria for question inclusion, see Stimson (1991).

[10] And in a few instances such series were created. See, for instance, Baumgartner, DeBoef, and Boydstun (2008); Kellstedt (2003).

type of disaggregation. More than two decades later, however, the dataset now consists of well over 300 survey questions administered more than 7,000 times at the publishing of this Element, the largest collection of public opinion data of its kind.[11] Such massive numbers create a new opportunity, one unprecedented in the field of political science – the estimation of multiple policy moods. We now have the ability to disaggregate mood and estimate longitudinal public opinion in more than sixty policy domains. And we have done exactly this: from military spending to health care to gun control to abortion, we now have a clear read on the evolution of public attitudes.

To estimate these series required a method for disaggregating the mood database. As a first step, and in an attempt to provide as many policy-specific series as possible, we began by matching each of the individual survey questions to a topic from the Policy Agendas Project Codebook (www.comparativeagendas.net/). For multi-dimensional questions, those that tapped more than one policy area, we assigned multiple codes. For questions without a clear link to a Policy Agendas code, we assigned a new code.[12] Those data – more than sixty "precooked" series – are now available to scholars via the Comparative Agendas website. These data also provide the starting point for our theoretical and empirical project in this Element and we discuss their creation below. We then discuss our selection criteria for a subgroup of series – twenty-seven series that meet a more rigorous standards for "thickness" (number of survey items that make up a given series) and longevity (number of years of data available) – that we analyze throughout this Element.

1.4.1 Creating Policy-Specific Mood Series

Once the raw items in the database were coded by the Agendas Project policy coding scheme, all that was required was to employ the dyad ratios algorithm (Stimson 2018) for dimensional analysis to a selection of items (by policy codes) to generate each of the possible output series. There is a mismatch between the topics government chooses to attend to (the basis of the policy agendas codes) and the questions survey organizations choose to pose. Thus, the usable, "precooked" series available on the Comparative Agendas site are created for the subset of policy codes where data richness permits estimation.

---

[11] These figures represent data collection through the inclusion of 2018 survey data.

[12] New codes were used for simplicity in the estimation phase, but will not appear in the Policy Agendas Codebook. We also identify these series by alphabetic names. See the appendices for coding details. Full details are available at our dedicated book website: http://fbaum.unc.edu/books/Opinion/Opinion.htm.

A usable series, by our criteria for the Agendas database, is one that (1) covers a reasonable time span (ten years or more), and (2) contains enough survey items to generate reliable and valid estimates. These decisions were made on a case-by-case basis, with two main guiding rules. First, in the case that a policy-specific mood series contains a small number (1–3) of survey questions, these items must be high quality measures of the concept we wish to tap. For example, there are two survey questions with Policy Agendas Code 1211, "Riots and Crime Prevention." One item asks respondents to place themselves on a scale determining the best way to deal with the problem of urban unrest and rioting. One end of the scale claims it is more important to use all available force to maintain law and order, no matter what results, while the other end claims it is more important to correct the problems of poverty and unemployment that give rise to the disturbances. The second survey item asks respondents whether the government is spending too much, too little, or the right amount on the rising crime rate. These two items do a decent job of capturing the mood of respondents in the arena of riots and crime prevention, despite the small number of questions used to achieve the task.

Because excessive gaps in question administrations alter the mood estimates, gaps of more than five years are not tolerated, and "precooked" series are not estimated. For example, a survey house may ask a specific question in 1960, but then not ask the question again until 1970. If this question series is our only source of data for the early part of the series (1960–1970), we simply drop this portion of the mood series. In the case of missing data, the dyad ratios algorithm interpolates data to generate estimates for the missing years. In cases of excessive missing cases (more than five years) such as these, we cannot guarantee the quality of the estimates and do not report them. Such gaps, however, are rare in our data.

Many of the series we create are more narrowly focused than are the Policy Agendas subtopic codes. In the Agendas coding, for instance, handgun control is combined with rights of police officers during internal investigations and with police misconduct issues. To clarify that our measure of attitudes toward gun control does not include attitudes toward the additional issues contained within this subtopic, we generate a new series for this narrower topic of handgun control.

Using this method, we are able to decompose mood into more than sixty policy-specific mood series, covering a wide range of issues. The value of such data to scholars of various fields is evident. First, instead of using global policy mood as a stand-in for all policy-specific studies, scholars will be able to tap into public opinion in their particular area of interest. Detailed diagnostic information is provided for each of the estimated series, including number of questions used to estimate the series, number of administrations, question wording, and survey item loading in the dyad ratios algorithm.[13] These data provide the user with a thorough map of how series are generated and what aspects of public opinion are exploited to estimate our policy-specific series. Moreover, item loadings diagnostics allow users to identify precisely which aspects of attitudes define and dominate their policy mood series.

Lastly, and most importantly for our purposes here, disaggregation affords us the opportunity to look deeper into the nature of public opinion, which we begin in the next section.[14] As noted above, we did not start with the denominator of all sixty plus series. Or rather, we did, but we narrowed our scope given our goals. We aim here to say something meaningful about the nature of public opinion dynamics, to build upon the important work of others, and to add our own theoretical claims. To do that, we must have public opinion data that spans more than just ten, or even twenty, years. Instead, we need to know the nature of public opinion over many decades. As such, we set our minimum requirement for policy specific series evaluation in this study to forty years. Doing so leaves us with twenty-seven series for categorization and analysis.

For better accessibility, we shed the Policy Agendas numerical coding system, and give our series thematic names. Tables 1, 2, and 3 list these series by name and provide an overview of the types of questions used to create them. The tables also include the authors' categorization of each series (either partisan, nonpartisan, or cultural shift), which is discussed below.

1.5 Categorizing Issues

Our distinction between partisan and nonpartisan issues is whether one could say that, over the entire post-war period, these issues have *regularly and consistently* divided the parties. Those that meet these criteria should elicit an implied thermostatic response. Those that do not should not. We have called upon our judgment as professional political scientists to identify these issues based upon the degree to which the two political parties regularly square off to contest them. Mostly those judgments are both easy and obvious. The majority of these issues are domestic ones related to New Deal and Great Society programs – programs championed by "pro-government" Democrats and decried by "small-government" Republicans. Questions about unemployment policies,

---

[13] See our dedicated book website: http://fbaum.unc.edu/books/Opinion/Opinion.htm.

[14] Note that the linkage of opinion series with government activity is an item of obvious interest, and our database on policy-specific mood, combined with the others made available through the Comparative Agendas Project, could allow such analyses. We do not explore these linkages here, as our focus is purely on developing our three models of opinion change. But we encourage others to follow up.

Table 1 Issue series analyzed

Topic	Summary of questions	Authors' classification
Economy	Should government ensure that everyone who wants a job has one? Should government ensure a good standard of living to those who are employed?	Partisan
Inflation	Is it the government's responsibility to keep prices under control?	Partisan
Unemployment	Should the federal government create/protect/provide jobs?	Partisan
Federal taxes	Are federal taxes too high?	Partisan
School prayer	Banning books from schools and support for prayer in school.	Partisan
Healthcare reform	Twenty-one different questions about the role of government in healthcare delivery.	Partisan
Big business & big labor	Which is biggest threat to personal freedom/the country's future: big business, big labor, or big government?	Partisan
Labor unions	Do labor unions have too much power? Support/oppose Taft–Harley? Support/oppose various union practices and protections?	Partisan
Environment	Importance of environmental protection versus prices, jobs, and energy supply. Doing enough/not enough to protect environment. Spending too much/too little to protect environment.	Partisan

For the complete text of all the questions used in constructing these series, see our dedicated book website: http://fbaum.unc.edu/books/Opinion/Opinion.htm.

taxes, labor unions, and help for the poor, for instance, are easily classified as partisan issues. Others deal with prominent and highly politicized social issues, such as abortion and contraception, prayer in school, and gun control. Together, these two types of policies make up the bulk of issues considered by Congress and the president and are classified by the authors as partisan.

Despite the large number of partisan topics expected to elicit thermostatic movements in public opinion, we anticipate a range of additional topics that will not. The issues in this category fall outside the scope of government

Table 2 Issue series analyzed

Topic	Summary of questions	Authors' classification
Crime	Should force be used to quell urban riots? Are we spending too much/too little on halting the rising crime rate?	Partisan
Marijuana legalization	Single question asking whether marijuana should be made legal.	Partisan
Gun control	This is a thick series with questions covering a range of related issues.	Partisan
Help poor	Spending for poor and welfare.	Partisan
Cities	Preferred level of spending on assistance to big cities.	Partisan
Scope of government	Do you favor smaller government with fewer services, or larger government with more services?	Partisan
Defense	Preferred level of spending on defense.	Partisan
Death penalty	Support/oppose the death penalty.	Partisan
Abortion	Thick series. Are you pro-life/pro-choice? Should abortion be legal under various circumstances? Should abortion laws be more or less strict?	Partisan

See note to Table 1.

framework and, for that reason, are not *usually* fodder for partisan conflict. In some cases, this is because the issue is not sufficiently politicized or salient to become attached to the scope of government framework in the American consciousness. Here, we have in mind issues like the management of national parks or funding for NASA. We also place social security in this category because the high levels of public support it receives from individuals across the ideological spectrum typically insulates it from political threat.[15] These programs generally enjoy similar levels of support from Democratic and Republican administrations and rarely garner national attention.

---

[15] Social security is a potential party cue issue, a Democratic program that Republicans itch to oppose. But because of its overwhelming popularity, they do not do so, neither actually cutting nor proposing to do so in their platforms. They express themselves as in favor of "entitlement reform," unwilling either to name the particular entitlement program they wish to "reform" or to use the more direct word "cut" for the reform they have in mind.

Table 3 Issue series analyzed

Topic	Summary of questions	Authors' classification
Drug rehabilitation	Spending too much/too little on drug rehabilitation?	Nonpartisan
General education	All questions are about federal spending on public schools.	Nonpartisan
K-12 education	About half are about federal spending. Others include public pre-K, vouchers, federal aid to build schools versus local responsibility.	Nonpartisan
Immigration	Should legal immigration into the United States be kept at its present level, increased, or decreased?	Nonpartisan
Social security	Assistance for the elderly. Most specifically mention social security.	Nonpartisan
Space	The right amount of spending on space exploration.	Nonpartisan
Gay equality	Includes questions about gay marriage, gays in the military, and protection against discrimination in the workplace.	Cultural shift
Black equality	The pace of change on civil rights, busing, housing opportunities, fair job treatment, and affirmative action.	Cultural shift
Women's equality	Role of women in society and at home and workplace discrimination and affirmative action.	Cultural shift

See note to Table 1.

Other issues are not sufficiently nationalized to respond to changes in party control in Washington. Kindergarten through grade 12 education, for instance, is primarily funded and administered by state and local governments, placing it outside debates about the size and scope of the federal government. Certainly there have been moments when educational issues divided the parties, particularly on the issue of desegregation. But more typically, partisans at the federal level have taken similar approaches to education. Similarly, public drug rehabilitation programs are largely administered by state and county-level authorities and have not been politicized at the national level. Conversely, international issues like US involvement in the United Nations and immigration policy also fall outside the scope of government framework and have not regularly and consistently divided the parties. In each of these instances, forces other than party control of the White House ordinarily govern public policy and public preferences.

Most issues will be politicized at the national level from time to time. This has been true for social security, immigration, education, and so on, and any issue we might venture to classify as "consistently nonpartisan" could experience a period of politicization in the future.[16] In fact, immigration became increasingly politicized during the Trump administration, due in part to the hard-line policies implemented during that era. But over a period of time spanning more than half a century, this recent trend toward politicization is subsumed by decades of bipartisan action. In fact, as recently as 1996, major immigration reform was enacted in Washington with nearly unanimous congressional support (Atkinson 2017, fig. 6.2). This was the norm for most of the post-war period, and for that reason, we classify immigration as nonpartisan. Conversely, partisan issues can exhibit moments of bipartisanship, but this does not make them nonpartisan in the broader sense. There was widespread, bipartisan support for the authorization of use of military force in 2001, after the 9/11 attacks, for instance. But this bipartisanship was fleeting and attitudes toward the war on terror (among elites and the public) soon came to fall neatly along party lines. No one would classify defense as a nonpartisan issue based on the momentary agreement between the parties early in 2001, important as it was. Using this same logic, we have not classified issues that are only occasionally politicized as partisan. The issues we classify this way – and there are a large number of them – are the ones that generate conflict between the parties at the national level, year after year, throughout the post-war period. The consistency and longevity of this partisan divide is what is needed to create a party cue strong enough to allow citizen inference about the direction of policy change based solely on control of the White House.

1.5.1 Validation

Tables 1, 2, and 3 report the classifications we assigned to each of the twenty-seven issues examined in this Element. Some readers will question them. Since some of the distinctions in categories can be challenging and since it is always

---

[16] Indeed, when we began this project, we would have classified space as consistently nonpartisan, but the Trump administration and its Space Force changed this.

reasonable for readers to be skeptical of author judgments, we attempt a validation effort. We wish to know whether or not we have correctly declared issues as partisan issues or not. To bring data to bear on the question we pull out individual survey items from the issue scales and examine whether or not there is partisan alignment in typical survey responses. That is, we examine the degree to which individual partisanship explains policy preference for each issue where these micro level data are available. The underlying expectation is that partisanship will have a larger impact on policy preference when the issue is partisan versus nonpartisan.

Consider an example issue: healthcare insurance reform. Is this an issue which regularly sees the two parties opposed? We think readers who pay attention to American politics will mostly agree with our judgment that it is. But it is not wholly a judgment call. There are data about the degree to which the parties disagree. Respondents in surveys regularly are asked to say whether they support or oppose reform policies like Obama's Affordable Care Act. Since about two-thirds of survey respondents report an identification as Democrat or Republican, we can cross classify policy attitudes against partisanship to see if these partisans in the electorate see issues in partisan terms or not.

We start with scales of multiple survey questions by multiple survey houses at multiple times. To confront the survey data we need first to select one item from each scale. In doing so we attempt to maximize over three conditions: (1) the content of the item is typical of the scale (face validity), (2) the item is strongly related to the scale (given by loadings), and (3) the item is available for a large sample of times.

The growing polarization of issues and party in recent years is a threat to comparability here. Since all issues are more polarized in recent years than in earlier periods, it is important to have a sample of items from the whole time span to avoid confusing era effects with issue effects. To deal with the confounding of polarization and era we select, when possible, items that were posed many times. The best of such items are drawn from the cumulative datasets from the General Social Survey and from the American National Election Studies. These permit analysis of party alignment across respondents and years. Here, we collapse data from all available years into a single measure of alignment for each issue. For a handful of issues the best that we can do is one item from a commercial survey firm posed in a single year. Where we have at least one year of micro level data, an estimate of alignment is possible. Where we lack access to micro data, no estimate is possible.

Table 4 Partisan alignment by issue category

Alignment category	Average R^2	Cases
Partisan	0.0394	16
Nonpartisan	0.0136	4

Note: Coefficients are from averaging over probit models for predicting binary issue position (L, C) from binary partisanship (D, R).

Estimates were possible for twenty issue scales: sixteen partisan and four nonpartisan.[17] We wish to observe correlation between individual party identifications and issue stances. Our standardized tool for the assessment dichotomizes both the dependent issue position (left, right, or missing) and partisanship (Democrat, Republican, missing). We then perform a binary probit analysis, predicting issue position from party. We average across the items in each category (partisan and nonpartisan, respectively) and display the averages of explained variances in Table 4.

The results in Table 4 serve to validate our prior judgments. Those issues categorized as partisan show nearly three times the correlation of issue and party as do the nonpartisan issues. The overall level of the two categories, not high at all, is a useful reminder that the intense issue and party alignment of professional politicians is much greater than that of ordinary citizens. America may be more polarized than it once was, but the level of issue and party polarization is still not very high.

1.6 How Many Dimensions?

Those who are very familiar with our work might notice a glaring inconsistency. That is the question of how many dimensions it takes to organize macro issue opinions. In this Element we assert that there are three dynamics of public opinion. Partisan, nonpartisan, and cultural shift issues each follow different patterns of change over time. Other scholars suggest that there are about as many organizing dimensions as there are issue bundles. They expect, for example, that issues of environment will share one, environmental, organizing dimension. Issues of education will center on an education dimension. Taxes, again, one further dimension, and so forth. This is a conventional approach to policy analysis.

---

[17] Micro data were not available for the following series: economy, inflation, general education, K-12 education. Theory does not tell what to expect of culture shift issues, so we do not include them in this test.

But one of us (Stimson) has argued in numerous publications (most notably Stimson 1991, 2004) that domestic policy questions are organized by a single dimension, called public policy mood. This mood is understood to capture what we usually call ideology – a generalized tendency to support or oppose positions related to the main line of political contestation. That some people organize attitudes in this fashion is itself a conventional view.[18]

So, the question is one or many? Does a single, left-right, dimension organize views toward most domestic issues or does each policy domain require its own organization? The point may be argued logically by pointing out that liberalism and conservatism are associated with policy views across many policy domains. Liberals favor greater government involvement (both by spending and regulation) across the areas of education, healthcare, environment, and cities. Conservatives approve the opposite. So unless we are engaged in a game of pundit illusions, there must be a single dimension that explains part of domestic policy.

But the argument may also be made by appeal to empirical evidence. The measurement model underlying principal components analysis (and the dyad ratios analogue that we employ here) decomposes the variance in a set of indicators into three components:

$$\sigma^2_{Total} = \sigma^2_{Common} + \sigma^2_{Unique} + \sigma^2_{Error} \tag{1}$$

In a one-dimensional solution common variance is the percent of all variance that is shared with the first dimension, here interpreted as left-right ideology. The unique variance is the reliable variance that is specific to the indicator, here a specific policy domain. As an example, take education. The unique variance is all the shared variance in the education domain that is not shared with the common dimension. This would be considered something that ties together education items but does not tie them to left-right ideology. Error variance is then the residual, explanatory failure, due to the variety of errors present in the indicators.

We know from the many years of micro research on ideology – see Converse (1964) and Kinder & Kalmoe (2017) for five decade bookends – that the result must be a compromise. All that micro research tells us that there certainly are ideologues who subsume at least most of their policy views to the left-right dimension. And there certainly are non-ideologues who have no connections among their views on various domains. We study the aggregate that must

---

[18] The literature on micro attitudes is notably skeptical that such attitude organization is widespread (Campbell et al. 1960; Converse 1964). But structure is enhanced by the act of aggregation, so what is relatively rare among individuals dominates the aggregate.

therefore be a mixture of the two types. And mixtures produce compromise solutions, neither exactly one-dimensional nor exactly multi-dimensional.

Consider our set of partisan issues. When we solve for the presence of an underlying (left-right) dimension for this issue set we find one. It accounts for 27.3 percent of all variance. This is pretty impressive evidence that divergent issue domains with party cues are well structured by a single dimension, ideology of the left-right sort.

Ideology of the left-right sort is usually defined by a subset of issues, sometimes called New Deal or economic or welfare state issues. These are controversies over the proper scope of government activity in education, environment, welfare, healthcare and so forth. Liberals advocate more government activity, spending, and regulation in all these areas. Conservatives advocate less. If we restrict our analysis to this issue set, the evidence of ideological structure is even stronger: 31.4 percent of all variance is explained by one dimension.

So yes, we do find evidence of unidimensional structure. And while we can't say how high the explained variance would have to be to rule out issue area structuring, clearly 31 percent is not everything. So the issue of dimensionality has no decisive resolution in these analyses. Just as we have collectively done for five decades of political behavior research, we can alternately consider issues as *sui generis* or as parts of ideological packages. For some citizens some of the time they are each.

As discussed earlier, the single national mood measure is a valuable contribution, and it fits the data well. But, as with anything, it can be broken down further to explore the different component parts. In this research, we have explored three components of the global mood measure. The largest group, partisan issues, corresponds very closely with the overall measure. Nonpartisan issues show little opinion movement overall. Cultural shift issues move dramatically over long periods of time. These follow a different logic, one that deserves to be understood, particularly given the substantive importance in US politics of the shifts in gay rights, women's rights, and racial equity norms that these series document. A three-part theory of public opinion change remains very parsimonious, and we gain from this slight complication of the original model. But if we had to pick a single description of the process of opinion change over time, the overall mood measure would still be our choice.

1.7 Plan of the Element

In the remaining sections, we use the twenty-seven series detailed above to test the hypotheses outlined here. We begin with an examination of relative opinion change in Section 2. In that section, we test whether opinion cycles, stays flat, or trends for each type of issue. Of course, we expect to find cycling where party cues dominate, stability for nonpartisan issues, and trending where social movements lead to absolute opinion change. This is, in fact, precisely what we find.[19]

In Section 3, we move on to a close examination of the trending opinion series – attitudes toward equality for African Americans, women, and members of the LGBTQ community. Here, we make our way through these three issue areas, examining each one separately so as to dissect the component parts of the mood series and gain a better understanding of the driving forces behind opinion change. We also explore the relationship between public opinion on these topics and government action. Unlike the dynamics of the thermostatic cases, public policy and opinion on rights issues typically move together in the same (liberal) direction over time. Occasional cycling – which we might think of as temporary backlashes against changing social norms – is subsumed into the larger pro-equality trend over the course of decades. But this is not to say that the volume of policy change is correlated with the share of the public in favor of such change. In fact, we find evidence that the amount of policy activity on rights issues diminishes over time, even as the share of the public demanding such change increases. We explore this dynamic and argue that it reflects public consensus around ending de jure discrimination and disagreement over policies designed to end de facto discrimination. Finally, we examine the dual effects of within- and between-cohort effects on trends in equality mood. Our expectation is that both will have strong effects on the trends we observe – and we provide evidence to support this supposition.

Section 4 explores the importance of changing social norms for bringing about "absolute" opinion change. Finally, we discuss the implications of this Element for contemporary politics. Many of the culture shift issues discussed here have become highly salient in recent years and have seen the rise of new social movements like Black Lives Matter and #MeToo. These movements have, in turn, sparked backlash, particularly an increase in white nationalism during the Trump presidency. We conclude by delving into the political calculus of the Republican Party, arguing that its embrace of anti-equality positions during the Trump administration was shortsighted.

---

[19] For two of the typically nonpartisan issues, space and immigration, the series trend. But this trending is out of sync with social movements or other events that would lead us to classify them as "culture shift" issues. Moreover, the contours of these series do not align with control of the White House. As anticipated, public opinion on these topics is shaped by forces other than social movements or party control.

2 Implied Thermostatic Public Opinion Response to Changes in Partisan Control of Government

The fundamental prediction of the implied thermostatic model is that public opinion moves in the direction opposite to the policy stance of the current government. Now it is time to test that assertion. We need to develop a test for this movement contrary to the current government. We then expect this prediction to be true for the issues we categorize as thermostatic, and equally we require that the prediction not be true for the other issue types. We assess these twin expectations in this section.

2.1 A Test for Implied Thermostatic Opinion Response

We wish to develop a simple test of the idea that opinion movement is thermostatic, and responsive to changes in presidential party control – the key to our theory of what drives the thermostat. A natural starting point is to define movement as a year-to-year first difference, $\Delta y = y_t - y_{t-1}$ for all t. But the direction of our opinion measure is in the direction of liberalism. So we are half right to start: under Democratic administrations we expect negative first differences, capturing the idea that movement is away from the party in power. To make this work also for Republican administrations, we reflect our first difference scores by multiplying by -1 during years when the president is a Republican. For either party, negative movements now imply movement away from the party's position and positive movements imply movements toward it. Our expectation naturally follows: *the implied thermostatic opinion response will produce movement in public opinion away from the party of the president*. Our party-reflected first differences should be negative on average if the implied thermostatic response is operating.

Thus, all we need do is observe the mean of the party-reflected first differences score. If the mean is zero, then there is no evidence of thermostatic response. If it is negative, then there is. And if the mean is positive, we have a strange animal that is definitely not thermostatic. So, a simple test against a mean of zero provides the test of implied thermostatic response (ITR). "Party-reflected mean first differences" is a mouthful, so we will refer to the coefficient simply as the *Implied Thermostatic Test* (or Thermostatic Coefficient in Tables 5-8).

2.2 Partisan Issues

We begin with the issue series that we have classified as party cue issues – and therefore implied thermostatic response functions. These are the standard materials of party debate, New Deal scope of government controversies with

Table 5 Thermostatic opinion change test applied to consistently and strongly partisan issue series

Series	Thermostatic coefficient	t	p	N
Federal taxes	−0.683	−2.958	0.002	71
Healthcare reform	−0.667	−2.043	0.023	62
Defense	−2.185	−2.003	0.025	58
Help for the poor	−0.802	−1.943	0.029	54
Scope of government	−0.682	−1.717	0.046	54
Economy	−0.430	−1.659	0.051	62
Abortion	−0.376	−1.587	0.059	59
Big business & big labor	−0.591	−1.580	0.060	51
Gun control	−0.403	−1.296	0.100	59
Inflation	−0.333	−0.923	0.181	42
Environment	−0.243	−0.552	0.292	47
School prayer	−0.027	−0.080	0.468	54
Unemployment	−0.021	−0.059	0.477	50
Marijuana legalization	0.037	0.101	0.460	47
Cities	0.055	0.153	0.440	53
Crime	0.058	0.209	0.418	50
Labor unions	0.159	0.669	0.253	72
Death penalty	0.471	1.924	0.029	64

"Thermostatic coefficient" is the mean party-control reflected first difference. $\frac{\sum_1^T \Delta y}{T}$ With the normal negative sign, it expresses annual percentage change away from the party of the president.

the addition of newer issues such as abortion, gun control, and contraception that are prominent in the social issues dimension of party conflict.

We display the test result for issue series where established party cues are prominent; see Table 5 where we array eighteen series selected for series of length at least forty years. The series are presented in ascending order of the *t* values for each coefficient, from most negative to most positive.

What we see in Table 5 is what we expected to see. This issue set produces predominantly thermostatic response with thirteen out of eighteen issue series showing the expected negative coefficients (and four of the remaining five effectively zero), indicating public opinion movement away from the position of the president's party.

Figure 3 shows our annual public opinion measures for each of the issues listed in Table 5, as well as for a summary index representing the average of all of them (in the thicker line). The figure also shows alternation in control of the

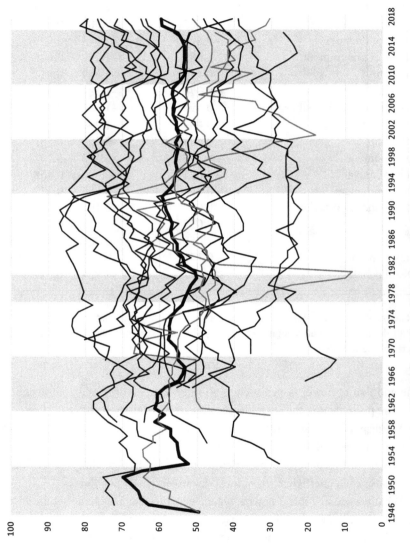

Figure 3 Public opinion dynamics on partisan issues

White House by shading in periods of Democratic control and leaving periods of Republican control unshaded.

We should note that one could write an entire book, a much longer one than this Element, attempting to tease out the idiosyncratic differences among the twenty-seven policy-specific mood series we have developed. After all, Figure 3 shows that some series have very low average values over time, some have high ones, and all do not correspond precisely to the overall index in their movements over time. Similarly, Table 5 shows that the eighteen issues listed there have very different thermostatic response coefficients, a few of which do not fit our theoretical expectations (and of which one is statistically significant). Rather than go down the path of exploring each of these eighteen series one at a time, or the twenty-seven series that we discuss throughout this Element, we focus on our theory. Our theory suggests that members of the public respond to who is in control of the White House and that public opinion moves in the opposite direction of that. But we expect this thermostatic response to apply only to partisan issues, not to issues on which the parties do not regularly and consistently differ. And we expect still a third model of opinion change, quite distinct in its empirical patterns, in those few areas where generational shifts in social and cultural norms overwhelm the short-term partisan conflicts on these issues. That is, we focus our attention on the main trends across the three types of issues that we identify. We recognize significant variation in the different individual data series that make up these three groups of issues, but we have no theoretical expectations about why they differ. Therefore, we leave the analysis of these differences within issue groups to others who might develop such a theory. We develop a theory about three issue types, not twenty-seven.

Can we make sense of such a spaghetti bowl? Table 5 gives a good place to start. The first variable listed there, Federal Taxes, shows a highly "thermostatic" pattern of movement systematically in the opposite direction of the party in control of the White House. Figure 4 shows the top four series from Table 5, those with the strongest thermostatic response; this is a subset of the data in Figure 3.

With some of the clutter gone, we can see the trends a little more clearly, and they show a zig-zag pattern over time. The different series show different levels of volatility: support for more defense spending varies quite dramatically, from as low as 10 percent to as high as 70; the other series show narrower oscillation. But in each case we can see that during the shaded (Democratic) periods, things are more likely to trend downward, and during the clear (Republican) periods, they oscillate back up. Table 5 shows that these patterns do not hold for each and every one of the series where our theory holds that they should, but the overall pattern is consistent with it. On partisan issues, the public moves in

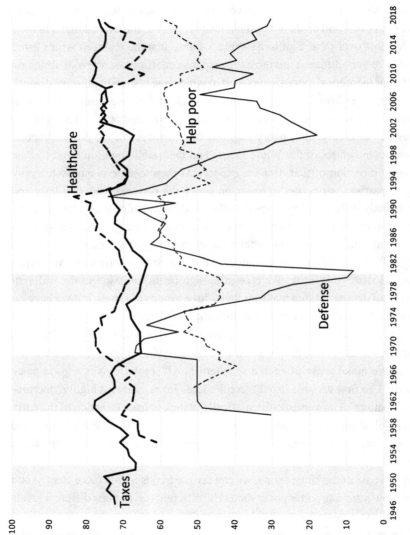

Figure 4 Public opinion dynamics on taxes, health care, defense, and help for the poor

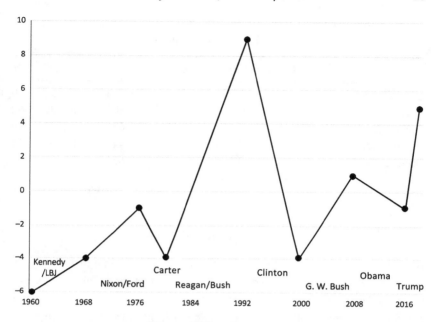

Figure 5 The zig-zag test

the opposite direction to the White House. We can illustrate this with one final simplification. Figure 5 takes the average of all the series presented in Figure 3 above. Then, rather than present all the annual series, it shows the value only at the end of each period of partisan control of the White House. Finally, rather than present the actual value of public opinion, it shows the difference from the previous period. This could be called the "zig-zag test." We expect opinion to move in the liberal direction (upwards) during periods of Republican control, and in the conservative direction (downwards) when the Democrats are in power. Figure 5 shows the results.[20]

When John Kennedy moved into the White House, our partisan index was at a value of fifty-nine; when Richard Nixon arrived eight years later, it was at fifty-five, four points lower. When Carter arrived in 1976, it was at fifty-four, almost unchanged. It moved to fifty at the end of the Carter years, then to fifty-eight in 1992 when Bill Clinton became president. When Republicans were in office, it moved up; when Democrats had the White House, it moved down. The zig-zag test does not fit the data perfectly, but the results are compelling.

---

[20] Values show the difference in the partisan index at the end of the term of a president from a new party compared to the value at the end of the term of the president of the previous party to control the White House. The series starts in 1960 because this value is calculated from the difference to the end of the previous Democratic administration, 1952, and we do not have data to the end of the previous Republican administration, 1932.

Table 6 Implied thermostatic opinion change test applied to nonpartisan or episodically partisan issue series

Series	Thermostatic coefficient	t	p	N
General education	−0.296	−1.814	0.039	40
K-12 education	−0.214	−1.305	0.098	62
Social security	−0.119	−0.650	0.258	40
Immigration	0.343	0.444	0.330	54
Drug rehabilitation	0.179	0.651	0.259	45
Space	1.102	2.279	0.014	45

2.3 Nonpartisan Issues

Next we perform the same test on a set of issue domains that historically are characterized by absence of party cues or cues that are only episodically partisan. Table 6 shows that only three of the six issue domains have negative reactions to current policy and only one significantly. Instead we see pretty clear evidence that party control does not matter.

Soroka and Wlezien (2010) conclude that it is public importance that determines whether or not the public responds thermostatically:

> We expect responsiveness only in domains of some public importance—that is, we do not (and should not) expect citizens to respond in domains about which they care relatively little. (Soroka and Wlezien 2010, 169)

Here we differ from Soroka and Wlezien. Our theory points to the existence of stable party cues as the causal force producing thermostatic response. But issues can be important without having stable party cues. To be fair, the two go together, of course. Issues *become* important when they are grist for party debate. And so party cue issues tend to be seen as important issues. Furthermore, we believe that the public's perception of the party – the expectations citizens tie to the parties (e.g., Democratic administrations spend more) – is the driving force behind the thermostat. This explains why, for example, we observe thermostatic response even when governments *are not acting* (Erikson et al. 2002). Party names provide quick cues on which citizens rely and use to make assumptions about what government is doing in areas where they are less informed. We are hardly the first to suggest the power of heuristics in politics (Dancey and Sheagley 2011; Kuklinski, Quirk, Jerit, Schweider, and Rich 2000; Popkin 1991). But this attention to party cues we stress also helps explain why we may *not* observe thermostatic response in some salient and important policy areas like education and social security: the parties' platforms

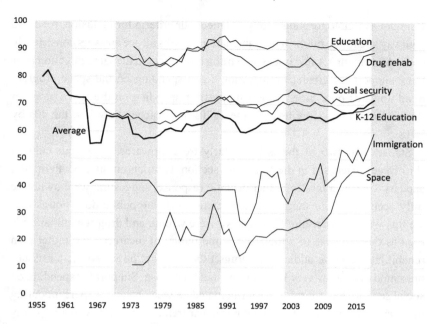

Figure 6 Public opinion movement on nonpartisan issues

do not differ in obvious ways. These domains are not unimportant, as Soroka and Wlezien's theory might suggest, but the public is not receiving divergent party cues either.

Figure 6 shows how public opinion on these nonpartisan issues has fluctuated over time. For each of the series listed in Table 6, it presents the time series of our mood measure, as well as a summary indicator representing the average of all the individual series (shown in bold). As before, Democratic periods of White House control are shaded in gray. While some of the individual series appear to move in different directions, on average there is no relation between public opinion and partisan control of the White House.

Many of the issues presented here have consistently high support among the public.[21] Compared to the partisan series, these nonpartisan issues have consistently higher public support (as evidenced by higher "liberalism" in the mood measure). We can see from Figure 6 that education, drug rehabilitation programs, social security, and K-12 education specifically never go below 60 percent support. (Similarly, though not included here because the data series

---

[21] This is to be expected. When there is broad support among members of the public for a policy solution, neither political party has an interest in taking a position in opposition to the public's wishes. High levels of public support can promote bipartisanship among political elites. Conversely, bipartisanship amongst members of the elite can promote support amongst members of the public (see Atkinson 2017).

were not available for long enough to meet our criteria for inclusion, road and highway spending, public lands, and national parks all see answers consistently above 80 percent.) A few issues see strong movement in the same direction over time: support for greater immigration[22] and spending on the space program trend upwards over time, though support for spending on the space program started from a very low level in the 1970s and reaches only into the 40s by 2018.

Statistically, two of the issues clearly trend upwards, as do our cultural shift issues discussed in the following section. Opinion on drug rehabilitation appears to show a moderate thermostatic response, suggesting we may not be fully accurate in our theoretical expectation that the public does not associate this with partisanship. (Perhaps we were wrong, and drug rehabilitation is seen as the converse to a tough-on-crime policy of incarcerating, rather than rehabilitating, those addicted to drugs.) On average, however, the six issues presented here show very little thermostatic response. Support for spending on social security and for the elderly fluctuated between 65 and 75 percent during the period displayed here, with no particular trend, and in a way that was only slightly negatively correlated with control of the White House. Our goal here is not to summarize each of these issues one at a time, but to note how differently they behave, taken as a group, from the partisan issues we analyzed in Table 5 above.

With political attention rarely focused on whether we support or dislike our national parks, public opinion on this topic, like the others in Table 6, cannot be expected to follow a thermostatic model. All of our nation's presidents and their party leaders have extolled the virtues of Smokey Bear, fresh air and exercise, and the beauty of what they sometimes refer to as our national jewels. Similarly, building roads and bridges, improving highways, improving the nation's schools, protecting public lands, safeguarding social security, and the other matters listed in Table 6 generate more consensus than discord. When there is discord, it is not systematically tied to the party system, at least not in a consistent manner over the entire post-war period. To be sure, the parties sometimes conflict over some of the issues listed in Table 6, including social security and immigration, particularly. They also often offer different proposals

---

[22] As anticipated, the movement in this series is not thermostatic. We did not expect public opinion to oscillate with party control of the White House because immigration has been a nonpartisan issue for most of the period studied. We find that from the 1960s until the early 1990s, opinion on immigration was quite stable. From the mid-1990s onward it has trended in the liberal direction, regardless of partisan control in Washington. Future research might investigate the causes of this recent trend. For our purposes, however, it is sufficient to note the lack of thermostatic movement in this series.

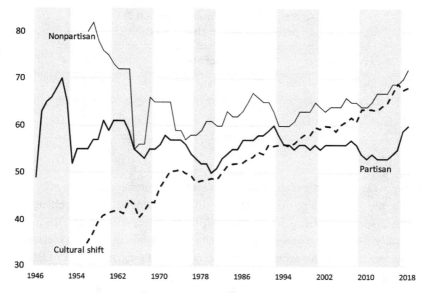

Figure 7 Three issue types compared

about how to help our schools. But over the entire historical period since World War II, these differences have either been muted or inconsistent for the issues discussed here.

To say that the implied thermostatic model does not apply to the issues listed in Table 6 and in Figure 6 is not a critique of the model. Rather, it is a statement of the limits of its applicability. The thermostat applies to issues where there is regular partisan conflict and where members of the public can make some inference about the current direction of public policy either by reading the papers, paying attention to politics or just by knowing who is in the White House. But where these indicators have no bearing on the matter at hand, such as whether we like our national parks or want to support the nation's schooling system, the thermostat is just not operable. Rather, aggregate opinion in these areas drifts, remains relatively stable, or sometimes shifts in a trend over time. Overall, however, as Figure 7 makes clear, our summary of all the series shown in Figure 3 ends where it begins, and there is no particular trend over time at all. The movements of these series cannot be expected to relate to partisan control of the White House. And indeed, the Figure 7 shows that whatever movements we do observe are unrelated to this question.

2.4 Three Models of Opinion Change, and the "National Mood"

Throughout our analysis, we have emphasized the general value of the thermostatic model, but that, since its driving force is party cues, it should not apply to

Table 7 Average change in public opinion at the end of
periods of White House control

Issue type	Democrats	Republicans
Partisan	−3.21	1.55
Nonpartisan	−0.23	−0.65
Cultural shift	3.48	3.23

issues where the parties fail to send consistently divergent cues, year after year. Along the way, we also noted a starkly different model of opinion change for issues associated with massive cultural shifts. Here, we noted that, if the parties typically differ at any given time, both are moving (along with the electorate) in the same direction, towards greater acceptance of the equal rights of Blacks, women, and gays.

Figure 7 takes the summary indices of our three types of issues, previously presented in separate figures throughout the text along with their component issue series, and presents them as one. The differences are clear.

We can see even more clearly the differences if we look at how the series changes after periods of common partisan control. Table 7 shows the average change in each series at the end of each period.

Table 7 presents a simple but telling test. The many individual series follow slightly different and sometimes idiosyncratic patterns, and the results from Tables 5, 6, and 8 in Section 2 above made clear that each individual series within a group did not correspond to the general patterns we have laid out (though most did, of course). But when we look at the partisan issues, values move down during Democratic control and up during Republican control. The same cannot be said of nonpartisan issues; there is no significant or systematic movement one way or another based on partisan control – both values are close to zero, and similar in magnitude. Cultural shift issues show increases in both periods; as they trend over time, this is to be expected. Over the long term, both parties, and the electorate, have moved strongly in the pro-equality direction. But at any given time, or during any given presidency, the Democratic Party has generally been seen as the one supporting greater social change in the areas of race relations, women's rights, and gay and lesbian equality. From this, we can expect that during Democratic administrations there may be greater normalization of these attitudes, leading to an acceleration of the shift during Democratic times and a slowing down during Republican times.

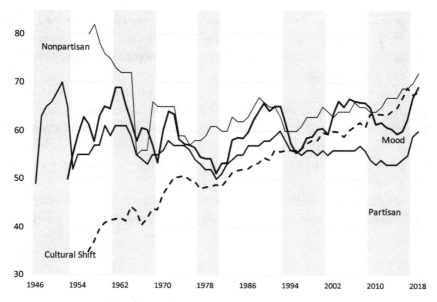

Figure 8 Three issue types and the mood

2.4.1 Three Issue Types Compared to the Mood

One of us (Stimson) developed the concept of the national mood and a methodology to measure it in a 1991 book and series of articles further developing the idea. It has been used thousands of times in a wide variety of scholarly articles, too numerous to enumerate here. We're attached to the concept of the mood, as we are to the idea of the thermostatic model. In these pages we have broken apart the component parts of the mood by looking at them one issue at a time, and clustering these issues into the three types we have described above. Here, we link these decompositions back to the big picture. Figure 8 shows how our three summary indices compare to the global mood measure.

The mood measure tracks closely with what we have called the partisan series. It is not identical, but the two series correlate very highly, and their correspondence can be seen clearly in the graph in Figure 8. The mood looks very little like the nonpartisan series, and completely unlike the cultural shift series, but it looks a lot like the partisan index; they correlate at .83.

We discuss in the Appendix an important phenomenon that affects our understanding of public opinion: public opinion polls tend to focus on the issues that divide the parties. Consequently, we have much more data on partisan issues than on other topics of public policy. A simple perusal of Tables 5, 6, and 8 makes this clear; of the twenty-seven issues used in this analysis, two-thirds fall into the partisan category. The mood measure, which takes all the data available, is therefore dominated by the series that relate to partisan issues; there are more of them available.

The thermostatic model applies quite well to the overall mood measure. As a general theory about the movement of public opinion, it's a winner. It is simple, elegant, powerful, and accurate. But in these pages we have broken out the mood into its component parts and found that we can complicate the story and recognize that, as good a theory as the thermostatic theory is, like any theory it has its limits.

We turn now to a small but important issue set that we have called cultural shift issues. It will turn out to have quite different properties than all of the others.

2.5 Cultural Shift Issues

Issues we refer to as cultural shift are undoubtedly *important*, but do not respond to changes in party control, and do not respond thermostatically. Three issues which fit this category are preferences about equal rights for Blacks, women, and gays. These three equality issue sets show, over time, trends indicative of absolute opinion change. As Americans become ever more supportive of equal rights for Blacks, women, and gays, they are not responding to the party of government.[23] Instead, each in its own way responded gradually to changing social norms, successful social movements, and important historical events. These stimuli, along with generational replacement, set into motion absolute opinion change on the individual level and at the generational level in ways we do not observe in other policy arenas.

Indeed, these issues are among the most important of our time. They are obviously salient in contrast to Soroka and Wlezien's position that salient issues are always thermostatic. We shall explore the trending behavior of these series below. This trending behavior in opinion change requires an explanation. Our explanation for these is that absolute opinion change – that is, permanent opinion change that is not responsive to changes in policy – is going on. Because these issues are largely unresponsive to control of government, the thermostatic tests of Table 8 are all nonsignificant and two of three of them are wrongly signed.

---

[23] In the case of rights for African Americans, we can detect some thermostatic response (Kellstedt 2003), but it is largely overwhelmed by an underlying linear trend toward greater acceptance of equality.

Table 8 The thermostatic opinion change test applied to three series associated with cultural shift

Series	Thermostatic coefficient	t	p	N
Racial equality	−0.244	−1.299	0.099	72
Gay equality	0.107	0.434	0.333	41
Women's equality	0.337	1.440	0.079	44

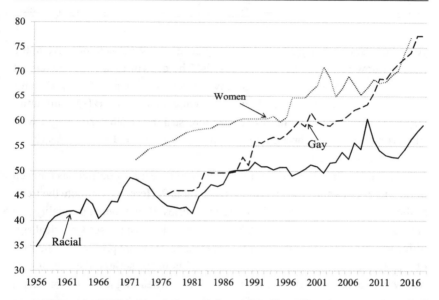

Figure 9 Racial, women's, and gay rights liberalism: 1956 to 2018

2.6 Trending Beliefs about Equality

Our contention is that racial, gender, and sexual orientation issues generate a different sort of opinion change: absolute opinion change, indicating shifts in underlying public sentiments. If we are correct, public opinion on these topics should not only fail the thermostatic test (as demonstrated in Table 8), they should trend in the liberal direction over time. Figure 9 provides a visual test of this hypothesis. It plots policy mood on the issues of Black civil rights, women's rights, and LGBTQ rights over time. The overall trend is unmistakable: the public becomes more liberal on these rights issues over time. Starting with attitudes toward racial equality, we can see over a half century of a trending process as illustrated by the solid black line in Figure 9. In the 1950s, about four in ten Americans supported equality as a goal and supported policies to end or reduce discrimination as a means. That support gradually grew over sixty

Table 9 Estimated trend coefficients for the three equality series

Series	Period	Trend coefficient	Standard error	*p* value
Racial equality	1957–2018	0.393	0.219	0.072
Women's equality	1973–2018	0.562	0.222	0.011
Gay equality	1978–2018	0.783	0.237	0.001
Culture shift (all three)	1957–2018	0.539	0.144	0.0001

years, reversing the majority and minority positions. What is impressive in the figure is how utterly steady the process is. The growth is like the movement of a glacier – very slow but very steady.[24] Growth in support for equality for women (represented by a dotted line) and members of the LGBTQ community (represented by a dashed line) is even more striking. Both series begin with support below or right around 50 percent in the 1970s and swell to nearly 80 percent support by 2018.

For a more formal statistical inference we estimate trend coefficients for each of the three series and display the results in Table 9. Here, we estimate the trend as the constant term for the first differenced series. Both women's equality and gay equality are easily significant, but racial equality just misses statistical significance. While mathematically this is due largely to more pronounced periods of backlash (evidenced by the downward shifts in the series), the substantive reality that racial equality does not reach the overwhelming levels of consensus at the end of series that we observe here for women and gays will come as no surprise to a student of US politics. We take this up in more detail in a later section.

Taken together, culture shift issues show an average annual movement in the liberal direction of about four to seven points per decade.[25]

---

[24] We can also see the thermostat at work in racial attitudes in Kellstedt (2003). In mood and all its correlates, the year 1980 is a conservative high-water mark. We see that too in racial attitudes. But here the movement is only *relative* to the steadily liberalizing trend, and because the trend is modest in speed, racial attitudes are highly correlated with other left-right attitudes, even though the one trends and the others do not. This latter finding is undoubtedly contrary to what Kellstedt may have predicted, but it appears to be merely an artifact of time. That is, because our racial attitudes series covers more ground than his, we are able to observe its trending nature in a fashion unavailable to his work.

[25] We investigate the possibility that survey question wording plays a dominant role in producing trending opinion series. In particular, it may be that we only observe thermostatic opinion movement when the questions themselves are worded in a relative manner (e.g., "Should the government be doing more, the same, or less?"). It may also be that in matters of equality opinion, all survey items are worded in an absolute manner (e.g., "Do you believe Blacks should have the right to vote?"). However, we observe no evidence of thermostatic (relative) opinion

Table 10 Estimated trend coefficients for partisan and nonpartisan series

Series	Period	Trend coefficient	Standard error	*p* value
Partisan	1947–2018	0.163	0.328	0.620
Nonpartisan	1957–2018	−0.199	0.902	0.825

As a final robustness check, we also estimate trend coefficients for the partisan and nonpartisan series. If our hypotheses are correct, opinions on these topics will not trend over time, and that is precisely what we find (see Table 10).

Substantively, these results demonstrate that the set of issues we have deemed consistently important to the parties, or even *sometimes* important, show no sign of trending.[26] In other words, they are unaffected by powerful stimuli like those that have influenced issues of equality.[27] Thus, we can now say with a large degree of statistical certainty that we have identified three distinct types of opinion change. In the next section, we delve deeper into a discussion of the forces behind trending opinions on matters of equality.

3 Absolute Opinion Change

Should an economic stimulus plan be passed in time of recession? Should assault weapons be banned? Should healthcare insurance exchanges include a public option? These are each examples of what we call absolute opinions. Each is presented as a fixed policy choice. This is in contrast to relative opinions which are posed in the form, should government do more or less of what it is currently doing? We assume that relative opinions represent fixed underlying preferences as compared to current policy. Absolute opinion refers to the fixed preferences themselves.

Support for civil rights for historically marginalized groups offers a prime example of absolute opinion change. First for African Americans, then for women, and then for gays and lesbians, American beliefs have evolved from a traditional status quo to a new belief in equality. The status quo, in all cases, was a traditional society which held that discrimination was the natural order

---

in many policy areas where the question series are themselves relative (e.g., aid to cities, public lands, space exploration; see Table 5). Perhaps more importantly, many of our survey items for the equality series are relative in frame – yet, we still observe absolute opinion change in the trending opinion series (see the Appendix for exact question wording).

[26] We also subject the three equality series taken together (as the "trending" issues) series presented in Figure 9 to this statistical test. The series is easily significant, $p < 0.008$.

[27] Of course, historical events may influence party control issues, but the impact of these stimuli are not lasting.

of things. Not to be too timid about the matter, most Americans believed that Blacks and women were biologically inferior, and gays morally inferior, all of which justified a society in which discrimination was both expected and normal – and assertions of equality were considered radical and deviant.

In this section, we make our way through the three issue areas, Black civil rights, women's equality, and tolerance and equality for gays and lesbians, taking on each one separately so as to dissect the component parts of the mood series and gain a better understanding of the driving forces behind opinion change. We also explore the relationship between public opinion on these topics and government action. Unlike the dynamics of the thermostatic cases, public policy and opinion on rights issues typically move together in the same (liberal) direction over time. Occasional cycling, which we might think of as temporary backlashes against changing social norms, is subsumed into the larger pro-equality trend over the course of decades. But this is not to say that the volume of policy change is correlated with the share of the public in favor of such change. In fact, we find evidence that the amount of policy activity on rights issues diminishes over time, even as the share of the public demanding such change increases. We explore this dynamic and argue that it reflects public consensus around ending de jure discrimination and disagreement over policies designed to end de facto discrimination.

Finally, we examine the dual effects of within- and between-cohort effects on trends in equality moods. Our expectation is that both will have strong effects on the trends we observe. We believe, for example, that a previously anti-gay rights individual may learn that a coworker that he or she respects deeply is gay, and thus, change his or her views on equality for gays and lesbians because of that experience. Likewise, many who lived through the emotional civil rights marches of the early 1960s, observing violent attacks on peaceful protesters, were moved to support civil and voting rights for African Americans. These types of changes represent absolute opinion change among individuals over time. Tens of millions of people really changed their attitudes. These massive individual level shifts in opinion play a significant role in explaining absolute opinion change (and, indeed, in altering the course of public policy).

At the same time, cohort effects may be powerful as well. As new generations come into adulthood, they have been collectively socialized in a time of greater equality norms compared to the older people they may be replacing. These elderly individuals were raised during periods of much lower levels of acceptance of these norms. So the engine of collective opinion change may have at its core the powerful dynamic of demographic turnover, and this may be further accelerated by individual attitude changes. One does not preclude the other.

3.1 Model of Absolute Opinion Change

Recall our demonstration of models of opinion change, which we now apply in the arena of social change. Again, we imagine an electorate with preferences scaled from left to right. Again, we ask the electorate relative questions, but this time, questions regarding equality for Blacks, women, and gays and lesbians.

Returning to the model of social change, enter the variable of time. Three results are possible:

A Over time, the electorate experiences no change in equality opinion.
B Over time, the electorate fluctuates – from more to less desire for equality – perhaps in response to changing party control, or perhaps to another stimulus.
C Over time, the electorate becomes increasingly pro-equality.

From Figure 9 (showing the three equality moods) and the trend coefficients reported in Section 2, we know we are in condition C. Over time, the electorate becomes increasingly in favor of equality. But there is one additional element to absolute opinion change: the question of who is doing the changing. Is the growing taste for equality an artifact of generational change? That is, is it caused by between-cohort change? Or, are cohorts themselves changing over time – within-cohort change? Or, is it both? We need to understand the moving parts of this condition C.

To answer these questions definitively, we would need longitudinal data (a single question or a set of questions covering multiple cohorts and multiple years) with thick responses (enough respondents to separate out the cohorts). Such data would allow us to produce a figure like the simulated image of Figure 10, which demonstrates both types of movement: between-cohort and within-cohort opinion change in equality beliefs.

Mathematically, Figure 10 suggests two sources of variation that explain over time change in equality beliefs. Cohorts themselves become more accepting of full equality – demonstrated by the upward trending movement of each cohort over time. And, each newer cohort begins at a more accepting point than its predecessor. Change is thus reinforcing, a combination of both types of movement. In other words, if we were able to break apart a single line of a trending equality series (such as the three core series presented above), we could attribute the trends to two types of change: within-cohort and between-cohort change.

Our statistical model for estimating the types of change is an analysis of covariance which simultaneously estimates the fixed effects of belonging to a particular cohort and the linear trends in attitude change within cohorts. The fixed effects are the intercept shifts of Figure 10 and the linear trend is the over time movement common to all cohorts.

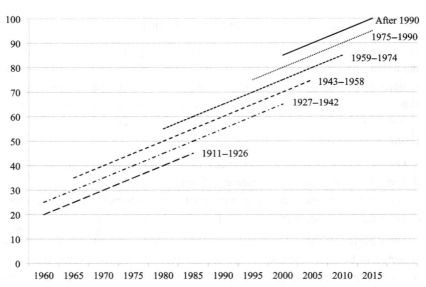

Figure 10 Simulated figure of percent of respondents believing in full equality by birth cohort

3.2 Generational Replacement

In all three equality areas, we can gain some traction on these distinctions. That is, we can break down our respondents by cohorts, or generations. The generational replacement hypothesis posits that earlier generations of Americans were socialized into a society where prejudice and bigotry were the norm (Schuman, Steeh, and Bobo 1985). Racial and gender hierarchies were clear in the 1940s and 1950s. Gay rights went largely unmentioned, at least publicly. Many in the majority did not think to question these norms. Later generations were socialized in an era where the three marginalized groups were more accepted. Thus, the hypothesis expects that as earlier generations are replaced by newer ones less exposed to overt prejudice, a larger percentage of the population will favor equality. The young then become the middle-aged and create a still more tolerant context for the next generation. And equally, the older generations who do not accept the changed views leave the electorate. That means that once a belief in equality begins to evolve, it is swept along by the tidal force of demography. As generations come and go, the public becomes more and more liberal in its equality beliefs, resulting in a steady, linear process of increased liberalism.

Before we begin the analysis of generational change, we wish to make a point about the measurement of racial attitudes. Recent scholarship considers the potential (and likely) effects of social desirability on survey response items related to equality, and specifically related to race, suggesting that as our political landscape changes and evolves, so should our measurement of attitudes (Bonilla-Silva 2017). In particular DeSante and Smith's work (2020) notes that while overtly racist attitudes may have declined, anti-Black stereotypes and racial resentment simply have not. This is particularly problematic from a measurement standpoint because evaluation of these critical attitudes has remained largely static and unidimensional. In response, DeSante and Smith developed the FIRE battery, which considers the multidimensionality of racial animus by capturing racial Fear, acknowledgement of Institutional racism, and Racial Empathy (2020), and provides a more comprehensive structural mapping of whites' racial attitudes.

One of the primary points these authors make is that younger cohorts know the "correct," socially acceptable answers to the standard survey questions used to assess racial attitudes – the very same survey items we examine. These findings are enlightening and validating for us. The fact that society now takes such a clear stand against overt racism that measures of it have become redundant helps to prove our point. Society has evolved. Sentiments that were once widely held by white Americans are now taboo. This certainly does not mean that racism no longer exists. It simply means that norms have evolved such that more finely tuned measures of racial animus are required to accurately capture it.

We do not require measures that are so finely calibrated for our purposes. We are writing and discussing an inherently longitudinal matter: opinion change over time, across a variety of issues. That means we require longitudinal measures, and thus we are limited by data that can carry and inform us across not just years, but decades. The measures we employ here meet that purpose. That is not to say we disagree with DeSante and Smith. On the contrary, we believe that the necessity of their clever and critical work supports our theoretical arguments and the findings we present. A social evolution has slowly transformed attitudes toward racial equality in the United States, and along with the tide of generational replacement, these forces have moved society toward greater racial liberalism.

We use survey items from the American National Election Studies (ANES) to test the generational change hypothesis. The criteria for item selection are (1) that the item be asked in as many studies as possible (to maximize number of cohorts), (2) that it share the trend of the estimated latent series, and (3) that it have face validity.

In the women's equality case, a single survey question spans much of the the entirety of ANES surveys. In the other cases, we have comparable items for shorter spans. We consider each in turn.

Table 11 Support for civil rights movement by birth cohort (percents are those choosing the responses "moving too slowly" or "about right")

Birth cohort	Percent support	N
1959 or later	74.8	1769
1943–1958	66.5	5277
1927–1942	52.5	4919
1911 to 1926	44.7	4689
1895–1910	39.3	2587
Before 1895	35.3	584
	Analysis of covariance	
Predictor	F	p-value
Cohort	60.96	<.0001
Year*	945.53	<.0001

* Coefficient on year, 1.31, standard error, 0.042
Source: American National Election Studies cumulative file

3.2.1 Racial Attitudes

We begin with racial equality liberalism in Table 11, looking to a survey item about support for civil rights asked from 1964 through 1992. The survey item asks respondents if they think that civil rights leaders are trying to push too fast, are going too slowly, or are going about the right speed. By combining the responses of "moving too slowly" and "about right" across birth cohorts, we create a measure of support for the civil rights movement, a critical aspect of racial equality.[28] The average share of respondents in each birth cohort that supports the civil rights movement is reported in the top portion of Table 11, along with the number of respondents for each cohort in the third column.

We perform an analysis of covariance to separate out the joint effects of (1) cohort differences, and (2) change within cohorts, displaying the results in the bottom portion of Table 11.[29] The racial attitude scores are predicted by cohort dummy variables (in the regression formulation) and by the year of the

[28] We are assuming a linear probability model for our dummy dependent variable here and in the following analysis. Linear is a close approximation for the range of values actually observed. The assumption aids interpretation and comparability with other analyses.

[29] In Table 11 and those to follow we present the raw means by cohort rather than estimated fixed effects. The two sorts of estimates are fundamentally similar, but the means are absolutely meaningful whereas the N-1 cohort effect estimates must be interpreted relative to the equation intercept and an omitted reference category. For background on the issues in decomposing cohort data, see Firebaugh (1989, 1990, 1992) and Glenn (1976, 2005).

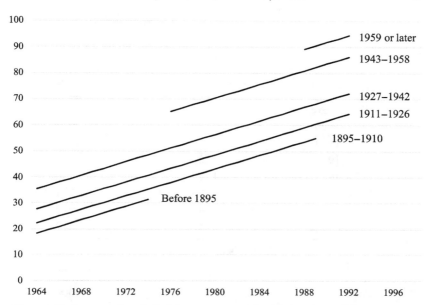

Figure 11 Support for civil rights movement by birth cohort (lines represent birth cohorts defined by year of birth)

observed response. What we learn from this analysis is that both sources of change are powerful. The cohorts are remarkably different, with almost Forty points separating levels of equality support reported by members of the youngest and oldest cohorts. Each cohort also becomes more racially liberal (at 1.31 percent each year) over time, resulting in about a thirty-seven point change, on average, for the twenty-eight year span of the question. This result could only occur if large numbers of respondents of all ages were undergoing individual changes, shifting from anti-equality to pro-equality positions.[30]

Figure 11 illustrates the results from the model presented in Table 11.[31] This graphic view of the findings of Table 11 represents what the somewhat abstract and esoteric coefficient estimates imply. The cohorts start out at notably different levels and all become more supportive of the agenda of civil rights over time.

3.2.2 Gender Equality

We are able to construct a similar cohort analysis for beliefs in women's equality using responses to an ANES item asking about the proper role of women

---

[30] See Firebaugh (1989) for a similar conclusion based upon different data.

[31] In this and two figures to come we choose to use all of our data for a single estimate of the upward slope of support. Thus the parallelism of the lines is an assumption, not an empirical finding.

Table 12 Belief in women's equality by birth cohort
(percents are those choosing the strongest full equality pole
of the seven point scale)[32]

Birth cohort	Full equality percent	N
1991 or later	70.2	285
1975–1990	62.3	944
1959–1974	51.0	4564
1943–1958	46.8	8660
1927–1942	37.2	5580
1911–1926	30.0	4731
1895–1910	24.5	1922
Before 1895	21.1	232

Analysis of covariance		
Predictor	F	p-value
Cohort	67.59	<.0001
Year*	338.33	<.0001

* Coefficient on year 0.626, standard error 0.034
Source: American National Election Studies cumulative file

in society. From 1972 through 2008 the ANES asked respondents to give their position on a seven-point scale that ranges from "women and men should have an equal role" to "women's place is in the home." The top portion of Table 12 reports the average share of each cohort giving the "equal role" response. The bottom portion of the table provides the results from our covariance analysis.

It would be difficult to imagine more fitting results: as the cohorts get younger and younger, the percent believing in full equality grows larger and larger.[33] The difference between the pro-equality views of the youngest and oldest cohorts is striking – almost fifty points. The analysis of covariance shows that the secular change within cohorts is just as meaningful. Over the thirty-six year period for which data are available, the average change in support for full equality was 22.5 points within each of the eight cohorts. Although the magnitude of this change will not surprise any who have followed this issue, the contrast with typical public opinion series is quite remarkable. Echoing the pattern seen with racial attitudes, both the cohort effect and the change within cohorts are powerful for attitudes toward women's equality.

---

[32] The ANES last asked this survey item in 2008.

[33] Mayeri et al. (2008) present a similar analysis of attitudes toward traditional gender roles by birth cohort using data from the GSS. Their findings are very similar to the those presented here.

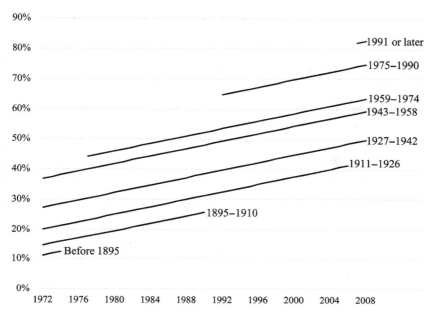

Figure 12 Support for women's rights movement by birth cohort (lines represent birth cohorts defined by year of birth)

Figure 12 is a picture of the relationships of cohort and time captured in the statistical relationships of Table 12. Again the pattern is that younger age cohorts start out more supportive of women's equality than older ones, but everyone (regardless of age) becomes more supportive over time.

3.2.3 LGBTQ Equality

Finally, we assess the impact of generational replacement on attitudes toward members of the LGBTQ community. We do so using a question that asks respondents how warmly or coolly they feel toward members of this group on a 100-point scale (i.e., a "feeling thermometer"). The question was first posed by the ANES in 1988 and was asked consistently through 2016. Table 13 reports the average thermometer score given by members of each cohort during this thirty-year period (in the top portion) and results from the covariance analysis (in the bottom portion).[34]

Once again, we find support for the cohort hypothesis: as cohorts get younger, the "warmth" they feel for gays and lesbians grows larger (see Table 13 and Figure 13). Cohort differences emerge strongly, with members of the

---

[34] We have considered the possibility that answering "50" may be evasive instead of neutral. We have done the analysis with those cases treated as missing. It does not influence the results reported.

Table 13 Gay and lesbian feeling thermometer by birth cohort (average thermometer score)

Birth cohort	Thermometer average	N
1991 or later	67.1	633
1975–1990	63.2	3888
1959–1974	54.0	7801
1943–1958	50.9	8974
1927–1942	44.9	4363
1911–1926	44.7	2210
Before 1911	48.9	439

Analysis of covariance		
Predictor	F	p-value
Cohort	49.05	<.0001
Year*	920.29	<.0001

* Coefficient on year 0.606, standard error 0.019
Source: American National Election Studies cumulative file, 2018

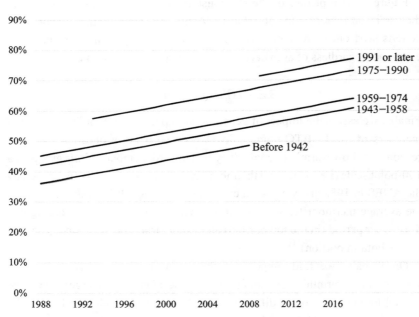

Figure 13 Gay and lesbian feeling thermometer by birth cohort (lines represent birth cohorts defined by year of birth)

youngest cohort feeling thirty points warmer, on average, than members of the oldest cohort. And, fully parallel to the earlier analyses, the change within cohorts, seen in the slope of year, 0.606, is larger still. As with women's equality, the large overtime changes in affect for gays and lesbians will come as no surprise to those who track American public opinion. Indeed, the crossover from minority to majority support for gays and lesbians has captured much public attention, most notably following the call for equal marriage rights by President Obama in his tenure in the White House, the first president to publicly do so. Note also that for all three cases the cohort progression is monotonic. With one small exception no older group is ever more liberal on any of the three issues than is a younger group. These are the raw data speaking. The power is in the reality of cohort and secular change.

3.3 Government Action on Equality

Although convinced by the support for our generational change theory, we are perplexed by a more normative question – why isn't the government doing more to ensure equality, given that public support for equality appears to be so high and to be increasing so regularly? For issue areas like health and welfare, public attitudes and government action move together through time, each influencing the other (see Erikson, MacKuen, and Stimson 2002). Yet for equality, we do not observe the same relationship between public mood and government action. That is not to say, of course, that the government has done nothing. In the case of equality for Black Americans and women, the government was highly active during the 1960s and 1970s, passing landmark legislation like the Civil Rights Act of 1964, the Voting Rights Act of 1965, and Title IX in 1972. Since then, however, government action has decreased while public support for equality has continued to rise. In the case of gay rights, government action has been more recent, including the passage of federal hate crimes legislation in 2009 and the landmark *Obergefell* v. *Hodges* ruling in 2015 (establishing marriage equality), but significant inequalities remain.

Much has been written about the history of government action in the three areas of equality we evaluate. For that reason, we do not provide a thorough review of that history here. Instead, we turn our attention to the contours of public opinion on equality. The thickness of the policy-specific mood series we have developed allows us to gain traction on this disconnect by teasing out the differences in public opinion toward *equality of opportunity* versus *equality of outcomes*, as well as differences in attitudes toward equality in the public versus private domain. As we will demonstrate, there is a significant degree of variation in attitudes across these various contexts, which may influence government responsiveness.

3.3.1 The disconnect between government action and public opinion

Despite various victories in each of the realms we evaluate, inequities continue to persist (in the form of higher rates of poverty and incarceration among African Americans, the wage gap that disadvantages women, the lack of federal anti-discrimination policies for LGBTQ Americans, and so on), while our collective belief in equality grows. What explains this disconnect?

In the case of gender equality, Sapiro and Conover (2001) argue that favoring equality as a normative value is fundamentally different than favoring specific policies designed to achieve equality:

> Whether individuals "favor" gender equality (a normative principle or value) does not tell us whether they believe that equality now exists (a perception) or even whether they endorse specific programs for achieving equality (policy preferences). The relationships among normative principles, perceptions, and policy preferences is complicated. The long train of public opinion research suggests considerable slippage between normative principles and behavior... (p. 7).

Due to the "slippage" described by Sapiro and Conover (2001), we can not treat belief in equality as a normative value as interchangeable with a pro-equality policy preference. This is particularly true because many pro-equality policies emphasize equality of *outcomes* rather than equality of *opportunity*. And while equality of opportunity is the touchstone of a liberal society (i.e., all Americans are entitled to the pursuit of life, liberty and happiness), the right to equality of outcomes has not been equally embraced by Americans. Once equality of opportunity is significantly advanced, or de jure equality is established, public support for further government action focused on equalizing outcomes may not exist, or at least wanes significantly. This is, perhaps, why we are observing significant activity on the topic of gay rights now – de jure equality has yet to be achieved but public opinion in favor of such equality has reached majority levels. For these reasons, we anticipate that public attitudes toward specific pro-equality policies, such as affirmative action, should enjoy less support than does racial equality as an abstract value.

Support for specific policies might also depend upon whether the policy calls for government intervention in the public versus the private sphere. For instance, Sapiro and Conover (2001) demonstrate that attitudes toward women's equality in the workplace, in government, and in the home are distinct.

Just because an individual favors equality for women in one of these three domains does not mean that he or she necessarily supports women's equality in other domains of life (although favoring equality in the workplace is highly correlated with favoring equality in government). Further, some research suggests that when questions prompt respondents to think about women as mothers, support for women's equality in the workforce is lessened. Mayeri, Brown, Persily, and Kim (2008) analyze responses to four separate questions about women in the workplace administered repeatedly by the GSS between the mid-1970s and 2004. When asked whether women should let men run the country and whether wives should put their husbands' careers first, the responses look nearly identical to women's equality mood. The series trend in the liberal direction over time and reach a level of approximately 80 percent liberal responses by 2004. But when asked whether it is better for women to tend the home and for men to work, and whether preschool children suffer if their mothers work, the responses are far less liberal and the slopes of the lines are less steep. While responses to these questions trend in the liberal direction during the 1970s and 1980s, by the mid-1990s the series flattens out with liberalism holding between 50 and 60 percent.

Based on the extant literature, we contend that it is the lack of consensus for specific policies that has resulted in the relative lack of government action on equality issues. We present evidence that speaks to this notion by paying closer attention to the survey questions that make up all three equality series – the component parts, so to speak. What we find is that the public is indeed far less supportive of equalizing outcomes than of equalizing opportunities. And lower levels of support for equality exist in the private as opposed to the public domain.

Another way of thinking of these findings is to consider the possibility that aggregate attitudes are simply less liberal than they seem. Americans may be more and more willing over time to answer in the liberal direction a generic question about the rights of different groups to enjoy de jure equality. But this should not necessarily be taken as a sign of support for government programs to do something specific to resolve issues of actual inequality. It could be cheap talk.

3.4 Deconstructing Racial Equality Mood

Racial equality, although long the topic of much discussion among scholars, was not studied in the longitudinal sense until somewhat recently (Carmines and Stimson 1989; Kellstedt 2003). From Kellstedt's (2003) work, we learned that racial equality mood has a cyclical nature, ebbing and flowing much like global mood. What we did not see from this analysis, however, was the overall *general* trending nature of racial mood described in Section 2. That is, with more data over a longer period, we see racial mood moving consistently in the liberal direction alongside its cyclical patterns (see Figure 9). This steady march toward liberalization requires an explanation, perhaps one beyond our generational change theory. While we have shown that cohort replacement motivates a large portion of change, we recognize there is more to be learned. We can attempt to expose more of the story by examining the questions that make up the series, thereby leveraging the richness of the data reported here. The racial equality series, for instance, is made up of responses to questions covering topics ranging from busing, to the speed of civil rights, to housing opportunities, to fair job treatment, and beyond. Parsing out responses to these various questions allows us to consider how the public views different aspects of the issue, and to observe differences in attitudes toward opportunities versus outcomes.

Previous scholarship, including the works of Sniderman and Carmines (1997) and Le and Citrin (2008) reveal that many Americans dislike affirmative action programs because they are perceived as attempting to *equalize outcomes* by providing preferential treatment to one group versus another on the basis of race. This aspect of affirmative action programs, Sniderman and Carmines note, actually violates the closely guarded liberal value of equality of opportunity in the minds of many Americans.[35] We might, therefore, expect less support for policies designed to equalize outcomes, as compared with overall levels of support for racial equality. On the other hand, issues related to government spending may activate considerations about the size of the federal government, and therefore, responses to them might exhibit cyclicality.

For these reasons, we chose to parse the responses to questions about racial equality into two new series and display them in Figure 14. The first is comprised only of responses to questions on affirmative action (shown with a dashed line) and the second is comprised only of questions related to "spending" or "doing more" to aid African Americans (shown with a dotted line). We plot these series against the full racial equality series (a solid black line). The figure reveals that when it comes to spending more and doing more to aid African Americans, we are, on balance, a liberal public, and are becoming even more so over time.

But note that the questions that make up this series are not designed to assess attitudes toward a particular set of government policies or programs, whereas

---

[35] As with most of the issues here, question wording also plays a role in levels of public support for affirmative action programs. Le and Citrin (2008) find that when questions about affirmative action refer to "quotas" for Blacks or women, respondents are less likely to support these policies.

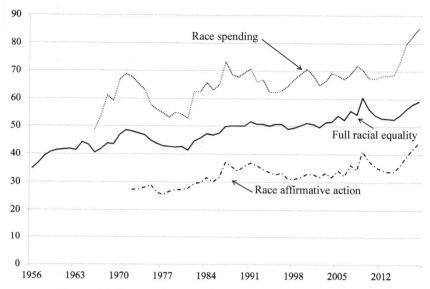

Figure 14 Support for spending versus affirmative action to
aid African Americans

the affirmative action questions are. Rather, these questions tap general attitudes toward increased government social welfare spending and, as a result,
they are highly correlated with attitudes toward spending on other domestic
programs. In fact, the large degree of correlation in attitudes toward government spending on different topics is the reason why global mood loads on a
primary dimension and moves thermostatically – when people want increased
government spending, they typically want it across the board, and vice versa.
As a result, the race spending series exhibits a greater degree of cyclicality than does the full racial equality series. Simply put, party politics do
influence responses here to a certain extent. Were this the only dynamic at
work, the series would be stationary. With the benefit of nearly sixty years of
data, we can see that it is not. Even with the presence of party-driven cyclicality, the series has moved gradually in the liberal direction over time as
social norms have evolved. Additionally, this series exhibits a greater degree
of cyclicality (at least to the naked eye) than does the full racial equality
series. When it comes to affirmative action, we see a very different picture:
perpetually low levels of support for outcome equality. Indeed, support for
affirmative action policies never reaches a majority level during the period
for which data are available. As a result, the full racial equality series (which
includes the affirmative action questions) does not trend as strongly as the
spending series alone, and does not reveal such widespread support for racial
equality.

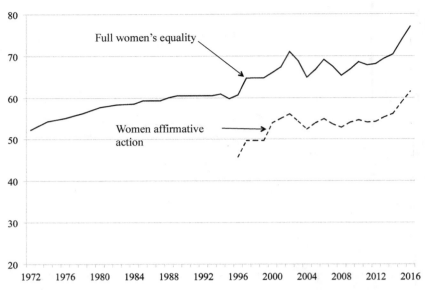

Figure 15 Attitudes toward women's equality issues (pro-equality),
1972–2016

3.5 Deconstructing Women's Equality Mood

The graph for attitudes toward women's equality in society and the workplace is strikingly similar to that for racial equality and, as we will see, for sexual orientation as well. Our full series for women's equality is composed of two types of questions. The first is related to women's role in society, asking whether women should be equal with men in industry and business or whether "a woman's place is in the home." Secondly, the series includes responses to questions about hiring practices that ask whether past discrimination should lead to special efforts to hire and promote women.[36] This second set of questions is clearly designed to elicit opinions on affirmative action policies aimed at aiding women in the workforce. We use these questions to construct a "women's affirmative action" opinion series and graph it against the overall women's equality series (see Figure 15). Doing so reveals that support for equalizing outcomes via affirmative action policies is consistently lower than support for women's equality in society. Nevertheless, the affirmative action series displays the same liberal trend as the overall series.

---

[36] One version of this question prompts the respondent to remember that "special efforts" to hire and promote women may discriminate against men. This question wording significantly affects levels of support for such policies.

Figure 16 Attitudes toward gay rights (liberalism), 1972–2018

3.6 Deconstructing Gay Rights Mood

The issue of gay rights is distinct from that of racial equality and women's rights in that de jure equality has not been widely established. For instance, there are no federal statutes explicitly prohibiting discrimination on the basis of sexual orientation in housing, hiring, or the workplace. The debate over equality of opportunity versus outcomes is, therefore, somewhat premature in this instance. Instead, public opinion on gay rights is more likely to diverge based on whether the focus is on establishing equality in the public or the private sphere. For instance, Egan, Persily, and Wallsten (2008) observe that attitudes toward gays in the workforce and the military (the public domain) have liberalized more rapidly than has public acceptance of gay marriage and gay sex (the private domain). Our data allow us to explore this concept by decomposing attitudes toward gay rights in three separate domains: the workplace, the military, and gay marriage and adoption.

The time series measuring support for gay rights is the shortest of the three equality measures presented here, but the trend is quite similar (see the black line in Figure 16). Since the late 1970s, when public attention to the issue began to intensify and polling data first became available, the public has become steadily more liberal in its attitudes toward gay men and lesbians. While we do find some evidence of thermostatic response, as we do in racial equality mood, the liberal trend is unmistakable. Each of the three distinct facets of the issue that we measure also trends in the liberal direction, but the slopes of the three series differ. Support for gay and lesbian equality in the workplace has been strong since the ANES began asking questions about the issue in 1977. It ranges from roughly 60 percent at the series' inception to nearly 95 percent in 2016 (the last year for which data are available). Public support for gays in the military has changed even more dramatically over time. When polling on the issue began in 1993, support for equality in the military stood at 45 percent. By the late 1990s, however, support had surged to above 70 percent. This spike seems to be motivated by President Clinton's promise of fully equal treatment before and during the 1992 campaign, which undoubtedly motivated public discussion and ultimately, the rethinking of attitudes about gays in the military. Since the mid-1990s support for gays in the military has continued to increase. Finally, while support for gay marriage and adoption also trends in the liberal direction, the public remains much more divided on this facet of gay rights.

3.7 Belief and Action: Concluding Observations about Equality

What we have observed, first with race, then with gender, and then with sexual orientation, is strong and quite uniform evidence of growing support for equality. Such trends started at different times and proceeded from different levels, but the similarity of trends toward support for equality is striking.

One might think that such changing public opinion would be accompanied by equally strong trends in actual equality. And there is some evidence for such gains. But gains in actual equality do not match the near uniform support for equality that we see in the public opinion data – nor is there much reason to expect gains in the near future. African Americans still suffer the disadvantages of relative poverty and mass incarceration. The 2020 Covid-19 pandemic has laid bare consistent and overwhelming disparities in health-care outcomes by racial group, as well as huge disparities by social and economic class. Women still face a glass ceiling in the workplace, are still subjected to sexual violence and sexual harassment, and are still underrepresented in almost all levels of government. LGBTQ Americans continue to face discrimination in numerous aspects of life, and new legal barriers to trans rights have been erected (such as barring trans people from military service).[37] While these remain true, there is little discussion of further policy steps toward equality, and there is little action.

Why is it that growing support for equality is not matched by equally growing evidence of equality? To answer that question we need to dig into what respondents are saying when they answer survey questions about equality. When we

---

[37] The ban was imposed by the Trump administration, but quickly reversed after the transition to the Biden administration.

do, we quickly see that two sorts of survey questions are widely employed. One is the question of goals, e.g., should women and African Americans have an equal role in society and the workplace? The second concerns proposals to eliminate discrimination of various kinds that is currently practiced.

What we learn from these question formats is that public opinion is more divided that it first appears. Decomposing the three equality series shows that (1) full equality is a goal that is endorsed by most, (2) most wish to remove existing forms of discrimination, even though they were once culturally accepted practices, but (3) Americans are not unified in support of programs that would actively produce more equal outcomes. Affirmative action programs lack majority support, let alone consensus. This is the only type of policy designed to equalize outcomes for which we found sufficient data to construct a measure. But by and large we lack evidence of support for measures that would produce actual equality because few such measures are ever seriously proposed and the issues do not become the subject of survey questions. So we know that there is a consensus on the desirability of equality as a social goal and a consensus that discrimination which would prevent equality should be eliminated. But we do not observe evidence of support for policies that would actually produce equal outcomes.

One can frame this discrepancy as inconsistent at best, cynical at worst. If citizens *really* believe in equality, should they not also support programs designed to produce it? Isn't it disingenuous to claim to support equality and be unwilling to take the next step and produce it? Here we encounter a pattern that is quite normal in American opinion and values. That is the fundamental belief in individualism, in getting ahead on one's own, that frowns upon measures designed to produce equality of outcomes. American opinion wants individuals to have to strive and struggle to attain goals such as equality. It doesn't believe that barriers should limit the possibilities. But it also doesn't believe that actual social assistance should help some to be equal with others. This is seen across the board in opinion studies.

On the matter of income, for example, Americans are concerned about and do not like growing inequality, and that carries over to weak majority support for a redistributive income tax system. But more direct measures that would produce more equality of incomes often fail to gain majority support. And so it is with social equality issues, such as race, women, and gay rights. The true consensus is for elimination of barriers to equality. But that does not extend into support for policies – for example, quotas of any kind – that produce equal outcomes.

So is opinion inconsistent and cynical? We take the opposite approach and conclude that were survey respondents asked the tough questions about policies to produce actual equality, they would in large numbers say no, at least to those proposals, such as affirmative action, that have been seriously debated and are the objects of significant public opinion research. It could be that opponents to policies designed to promote equality are better at bringing attention to potential problems with these proposals than supporters are in pointing out the cynicism of supporting the ends, but objecting to every means of achieving it. In any case, since this is an analysis of public opinion, we have to stop where we get to the end of what the public opinion data can support. Others will need to carry this question further with other approaches and other data sources.

4 Conclusion

In these pages we have developed policy-specific moods on numerous topics. We have laid out a three part theory that explains the forces that move these opinions to change over time. Here we reflect on two themes that arise from our work: what opinion change looks like in long-term perspective and how equality fits in the party system.

4.1 Opinion Change over the Long Term

Let's play Rip van Winkle for a moment and consider a hypothetical US voter from an earlier generation, perhaps someone who was already a mature voter in the 1950s. How might he or she interpret US politics these days? While public opinion on most issues we have studied has changed over time, this change has typically taken place within a limited range. For the first two types of issues we discussed, partisan and nonpartisan issues, we document no significant change in public opinion over the long term, but for the third type of issues, those associated with cultural shifts, we show transformative change. This implies that our hypothetical voter from the 1950s would likely have little difficulty recognizing the terms of debate surrounding such things as whether taxes are too high, whether the government is not doing enough or is doing too much in the realm of health care, regulating guns, dealing with unemployment, inflation, or other aspects of the economy, whether the government is dealing properly with the issue of separation of church and state, and so on. Things have changed, to be sure, but arguments about the appropriate size of government have a common quality. Similarly, for many of the issues we have referred to as nonpartisan, there are differences, to be sure, but a lot of commonality: the proper role of the federal government in K-12 education, how to maintain the financial solidity of the social security system, even the public policy response to drug abuse and drug addiction. Our discussions about space exploration might surprise, but not the idea that members of the public would be debating the proper role of US government in promoting the latest scientific advance, or the degree to which it should be spending taxpayer funds to do so.

Things would be different with regard to women's rights, LGBTQ issues, and racial equality. Our mature voter from the 1950s would never have seen a major party nominate a woman for a presidential ticket, and would not be accustomed to women holding important leadership positions in public, corporate, or academic positions outside of a few traditionally feminine fields. If our voter was from the South, most of his or her life would have been lived under the strictly regimented protocols of Jim Crow; schools were fully segregated and there were still separate but very unequal public accommodations for Black and white citizens. In sum, the racial aspect of public life would have been radically transformed. If our voter were from the North, the transformation of public life with regard to civil rights, voting, education, and involvement in public life would be no less revolutionary, even if starting from a different point.

With regards to gay and lesbian rights, most likely the hypothetical voter from the 1950s simply would not believe his or her own eyes. No longer was homosexuality illegal and held closely private, but the very laws of marriage had been changed to allow for same-sex marriage and child-rearing. These changes, even more than the others, probably would have struck our hypothetical time-traveler as most unexpected. Whether they were viewed as welcome or unwelcome changes, they certainly would be surprises.

What does this mean about the long-term nature of public opinion dynamics? First, though for our partisan and nonpartisan issues we show no long-term trends, our findings should not be interpreted to mean that nothing can change. After all, the answer to the question "Is the government doing too much, not enough, or about the right amount" to address a certain topic is based on some understanding of what or how much the government is doing. And our theory is that, for partisan issues at least, people infer that amount by which party controls the White House. And, both aggregate public opinion as well as government policy might move in a certain direction over long periods of time. For example, we spend much more today on Medicare and social security than we did in the 1950s, but the debate about whether we are doing "enough" or "not enough" remains seemingly eternal. The level of government effort at any given time, the status quo, changes over time, but the questions we rely on are phrased with the status quo as the reference point. So, substantial policy change can indeed occur even in a public opinion environment where individuals and the major political parties continue to dispute the question of whether the (shifting and evolving) status quo policy is too progressive or too conservative.

Similarly, we should understand that what may appear to be a dramatic or even radical reform at one point may become accepted as the status quo some years later. The creation of the social security program dates to before our public opinion series begins. But Medicare dates only from the 1960s, and was the subject of vituperative debate at the time, with allegations of socialized medicine flying about and much of the rhetoric being easily recognizable from today's debates about other policy proposals from the progressive side. President Obama's Affordable Care Act (ACA) similarly was seen at the time as a major step toward greater government involvement in the health care system. Today, Medicare is more the object of veneration and appreciation than controversy, and large parts of the ACA, such as the pre-existing condition mandate and the law's encouragement to engage in less expensive preventative care, are widely accepted and likely to be permanent parts of the health-care landscape. So, opinion shifts as partisan divisions continue. The reason is that the divisions surround a new status quo point. Fundamentally, for most policy issues we have studied, the political parties and the voters who support them still disagree about similar things. The items of controversy change but the fundamental divides among people that generate the controversies remain similar. Many of these relate to the proper scope of government. Even as the government has grown, that divide has remained.

But this perspective does not help us understand those issues that are subjected to the powerful social, cultural, and demographic forces that generate major changes in those policy domains represented in our analysis by the cultural shift issues. Here, we are not seeing the same debate around a possibly shifting status quo point. Rather, we are seeing real change. Much (but not all) of this change is driven by the motor of generational replacement. And while we have focused on the three cases with the best public opinion record so we can document these shifts, we can think of some others where the status quo, in terms of policy as well as in terms of expected cultural practice, would be unrecognizable to our hypothetical Rip van Winkle from the 1950s. Smoking in public places is a good example. Indeed, the rights of smokers were so entrenched that even private places, such as individuals' homes were expected to be receptive to the needs of smokers. In hospitals, few areas were off limits to smokers, except perhaps the intensive care unit and the surgery theater. In schools, teachers smoked in the classrooms. In universities, professors as well as students routinely lit up. Just as cultural norms have shifted dramatically in the areas of civil rights, gay and lesbian equality, and women's equality, there have been other domains of life where similar trends have taken place. So a full model of opinion change should take into account the importance of this third model, long-term cultural shifts in norms. These are moved along by the government, and the government is moved along by the shifting norms. Controversy surrounding the issue may remain and people may continue to disagree about the ultimate policy or state of the world that would make them satisfied. But there is little in common between these issues where we see decades of movement in the same direction, with little variability depending on which party controls the White House, and the partisan issues that dominate our study. Norms change over time and, while at any given moment it may not seem as though there is much opportunity for such changes, with a longer time perspective we can observe them clearly.

4.2 Movements for Equality and Partisan Politics in Contemporary America

Recent years have seen increasing public pressure for equality, which has generated large scale protests (such as the 2017 Women's March) and the formation of social movements like Black Lives Matter, Defund the Police, and the #MeToo movement. Pressure from these groups has exposed wrong-doing among elites and ended or derailed the careers of politicians, journalists, and celebrities like former Senator Al Frankin, former Congressman Steve King, journalist Matt Lauer, and actor and comedian Louis C. K. These movements are also helping to shape policies, particularly around police use of force, in communities across the country. But this public pressure and advances for women, African Americans, and LGBTQ Americans has also generated backlash.

Some celebrity activists, like former NFL quarterback Colin Kaepernick (who took a knee during the national anthem to protest police brutality), have seen their careers collapse after taking a public stand for equality. Others, like US women's soccer star and LGBTQ activist Megan Rapinoe, found themselves at the center of public controversies following similar protests. Conversely, some public figures charged with racism or sexual misconduct have ascended to the highest levels of government. President Trump is the clearest example. Trump frequently made both veiled and overtly racist remarks in interviews, tweets and speeches (Leonhardt and Philbrick 2018). During his 2020 run for reelection, he refused to denounce white supremacists during the second presidential debate, and he has been accused of sexual assault by more than twenty women (Zhou 2020). In 2016, these allegations of sexual misconduct did not hinder his successful presidential bid, and research shows that his racist and anti-immigrant rhetoric helped him with some voters. For instance, Hooghe and Dassonneville (2018) find that racist and anti-immigrant sentiments among voters were key predictors of a vote for Trump in 2016.

Once in office, the Trump administration pursued an array of policies designed to roll back rights for women, racial minorities, and members of the LGBTQ community. For the latter group, this included ending Title IX protections for transgender students, derailing efforts by multiple agencies to collect data on LGBTQ Americans and their needs, barring transgender individuals from military service, and altering the US Department of Justice's interpretation of Title VII of the 1964 Civil Rights Act by asserting that the law does not protect transgender students (Conference 2018).

President Trump, with the aid of Republican allies in the Senate, also pushed through the nomination of conservative judge Brett Kavanaugh to the Supreme Court, despite allegations of sexual misconduct. While Trump ultimately lost his reelection bid in 2020, he expanded his margin in the popular vote that year – meaning that Trump's rhetoric and anti-equality stance likely helped him expand his base of support. This political calculus helps to explain why few congressional Republicans have distanced themselves from Trump.

Given all of the evidence we have presented in this Element, showing the steady march of public opinion toward pro-equality views, why would President Trump and congressional Republicans pursue an anti-equality agenda and how could this strategy prove successful? The answer is that for politicians, who are constrained by the short-term goal of reelection, the slow pace of change in favor of equality makes it tempting to ignore long-term shifts in public opinion. The Trump presidency was defined both by pro-equality protests and by backlash against the gains for equality made during the Obama administration. Trump successfully tapped into fervent anti-equality sentiment and stoked those feelings among his loyal followers during four years in office. But this strategy, while successful for Republicans in the short term, is irrational in the long run. As our cohort analysis demonstrates, younger members of our society are far more likely to hold pro-equality views than are members of older generations. As these young adults replace older voters, it is very difficult to envision a path to victory at the national level for a political party that openly embraces racism, misogyny, xenophobia, homophobia and transphobia. Either the Republican Party will have to change course in the coming years and rediscover its pro-equality roots, or risk losing its ability to compete in federal elections.

Appendix
Comparing the Survey Research Agenda to the Congressional Agenda

Our analysis is based on a compilation of 355 distinct survey questions administered to national samples of US adults 7,217 times in the period from 1946 through 2018. The questions that pollsters find to be of interest tend to focus on hot-button issues that divide Americans (civil rights, welfare, the environment), or on consistently posed series of questions about such things as the state of the economy, crime, health care, and the environment. Because our study of how public opinion relates to government activity requires data on public opinion, we are limited by what the pollsters provide. Rather than happily but blindly assume that what they provide is what we would want in a perfect world, we believe it is important to understand how reality and perfection sometimes differ. So in this section we analyze what might be called the "polling agenda" and compare it with another, the "congressional hearings agenda." This is a list of all hearings that have occurred in the US House and Senate since 1947. Of course, we could compare the polling agenda to other agendas, such as the media agenda, the presidential agenda, the topics on which Congress passes laws, or the list of topics on which the US Supreme Court makes rulings. We simply take the congressional hearings agenda as one alternative indicator of what the legislative branch of the federal government is paying attention to. It turns out that the polling agenda is almost unrelated to the congressional hearings agenda.

In order to compare the 355 questions from the polling agenda to the congressional hearings agenda, we classified each of the polling questions into the topic classification system of the Policy Agendas Project (PAP). Because some survey questions seem related to more than one PAP category, we allowed for some questions to be classified into two PAP subtopics. For example, questions about what to do about drug addiction were matched both with a health care topic as well as with a criminal justice topic. This led to a total of 481 matches, counting these double classifications.

Figures 17 and 18 show the simple comparison of the two agendas. Recall that the congressional hearings database includes over 100,000 hearings from 1947 through 2017 and are drawn from the Policy Agendas Project. The policy

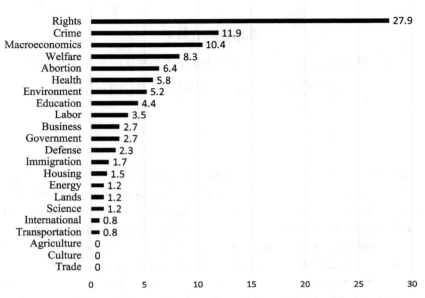

Figure 17 The polling agenda (based on 481 questions incorporated into our analysis)

topics are the twenty-one major topics of the PAP, with the additional topic of abortion added because of its high frequency in the polling agenda.[38]

Attention in the polling agenda is highly concentrated compared to that of congressional hearings. Over 25 percent of all public opinion polls entering into the mood database relate to civil rights and crime. Macroeconomics also has more than 10 percent of the total number of questions. These issues are much smaller parts of the congressional hearings agenda. However; they represent just 2.6, 4.5, and 3.5 percent of all hearings, respectively. In fact, the correlation of the two data series shown in the two figures is negative: -0.1570 to be exact. If, instead of the 22 major topics displayed in Figure 18 we look at over 200 more specific policy subtopics, the correlation is almost perfectly zero: -0.0353.

Should we be surprised that the polling agenda is different from the congressional hearings agenda? Not really. Congress does a lot of things, such as consider presidential nominations to various appointed positions or oversee federal agencies that manage public lands, which generate more yawns than protests among members of the public. Governments do a lot of things that are

---

[38] Congressional hearings touching on abortion, which perhaps surprisingly are relatively rare, would be coded as health care if they related to family planning and contraception issues or civil rights (privacy) if they related to *Roe* v. *Wade* and constitutional issues surrounding the topic. The PAP coding of abortion, or lack thereof, is due to how the issue is framed, or avoided, in most congressional activity.

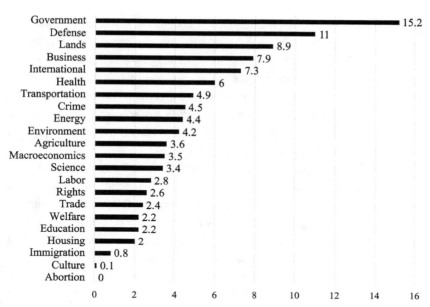

Figure 18 The congressional hearings agenda (based on the 100,056
congressional hearings from 1947 to 2017)
Source: www.comparativeagendas.net/us. Downloaded
May 20, 2020.

not of much interest to the public, most of the time. However, virtually any one
of these issues could potentially emerge as a publicly salient issue some of the
time. Most judicial nominations are handled quietly, but some Supreme Court
nominations generate high levels of attention, controversy, and public concern.
Most oversight of military bases and veterans' hospitals generate no interest
outside of concerned professionals or those directly affected, but occasionally
these issues can attract a lot of attention, as shown recently with discussions
of renaming US military bases named after generals who committed treason
during the US Civil War, or when there have been scandals associated with
mismanagement in the Veterans Benefits Administration. Public attention may
occasionally be aroused, and public opinion may occasionally be measured, on
such topics, but for the most part many issues are well below the radar.

Several implications follow from the disjuncture between the generally unin-
teresting (to the public) congressional hearings agenda and the polling agenda.
First, it should be clear that members of the public are not closely monitor-
ing congressional activities, and our theories of public opinion responsiveness
should be correspondingly undemanding with regard to assumptions about public interest in the government. Our key assumption in the implied thermostatic
model was that members of the public know which of the two major political

parties controls the White House. This is certainly a better assumption than one requiring significant knowledge of what the government is doing at any given time. (To be clear, we do not mean to suggest that most political scientists, or even very many, violate the assumption of low public interest in politics. Rather, this is a reminder to the reader, perhaps less familiar with the literature, that people pay much more attention to shopping, fashion, sports, and the weather than to what might be on C-SPAN at any given moment, with notable exceptions to this general rule.)

Second, we can expect that the polling agenda, focusing as it does on highly salient points of social disagreement, is tilted in the direction of what we have called partisan and cultural shift issues. Our cultural shift issues (civil rights for Blacks, women, and gays) certainly have been the subjects of a lot of public opinion polling; these were some of the highest values in Figure 17 above. And many of the bread-and-butter issues of public opinion polling, such as crime, aid to the poor, and regulation of business, are at the heart of the partisan divide. On the other hand, many issues in our nonpartisan category are simply not the object of a lot of public opinion polling and are therefore not in our database. We can only study what data are available, but we note here a restriction to our analysis and to any theory of public opinion; for many areas of public policy where Congress, the president, and various federal agencies might be spending money and engaging in important policy decisions, there is little public opinion engagement. And if there is, the polling firms and academic survey houses are not gathering it. The polling agenda targets issues that divide us. But governments do more than that; they often engage in policy activities that are not the subject of significant debate or conflict.

We are not the first to study how the polling agenda differs from other agendas. Jason Barabas (2016) presents a Venn diagram with the national policy agenda at the center, and asks the question: How much do survey questions overlap? Is there substantial, some, or minimal overlap? He then compares the iPOLL archive, a repository of over 600,000 survey questions and responses (and a key source of the data we use in this book) with Binder's 1999 study of the "national policy agenda," which she measured by coding policy-related editorials in the New York Times from 1947 through 2000. This measure identified 2,818 issues. Barabas then had coders review more than 20,000 polls from the iPOLL collection to see if there were relevant questions on the same issues. This procedure identified 658 issues, or 23 percent of the total. However, these were not consistently available over time. Looking over every two-year Congress, he found that relevant polling data was available for about one-quarter of the issues on the policy agenda (Barabas 2016, fig. 2, 446), with this value sometimes below 10 percent and occasionally as high as 35 percent. While his study reviews the substantive implications of this relatively low degree of over-lap for the study of public-opinion responsiveness, that is not our main concern here. Rather, we are interested in the Venn diagram indicating 28 percent over-lap, and the dynamics of that over time, reaching sometimes below 10 percent. Clearly, pollsters are not in the business simply of asking questions about what Congress is up to. Sometimes, they focus their attention on other issues, and sometimes Congress delves deeply into the policy weeds on topics where the survey research houses show very little willingness to conduct polls.

A second study that took seriously the issue of differences across agendas was by Frank Baumgartner and colleagues 2009, in a book-length analysis of lobbying. After assessing the "lobbying agenda" by looking at a sample of issues on which lobbyists were plying their trade in Washington over a four-year period in the Clinton and second Bush administrations (e.g., 1999 to 2003), they compared the topics on which the lobbyists were active with the topics mentioned in public opinion surveys asking people to mention the "most impor-tant problem" facing the country. They found very little correspondence. "At the time of our research, the top public concerns were crime, the economy, international affairs, education, health, and social welfare. The top issues our lobbyists were working on are, by contrast, health, environment, transportation, banking, defense, science and telecommunications, and foreign trade" (2009, 257). The issue is probably worse than it appears, because of the very precise and financial aspect of much lobbying. Health care, to the public, generally concerns issues related to the high cost and lack of availability of services. To lobbyists, it is increasing reimbursement rates for professional services. In sum, agendas differ.

For more information about our data, codebooks, and information about the book, please see our dedicated book website: http://fbaum.unc.edu/books/Opi nion/Opinion.htm.

References

Atkinson, M. L. (2017). *Combative politics: The media and public perceptions of lawmaking*. Chicago: University of Chicago Press.

Barabas, J. (2016). Democracy's denominator: Reassessing responsiveness with public opinion on the national policy agenda. *Public Opinion Quarterly*, *80*(2), 437–459.

Baumgartner, F. R., DeBoef, S., and Boydstun, A. (2008). *The decline of the death penalty and the discovery of innocence*. New York: Cambridge University Press.

Baumgartner, F. R., Berry, J. M., Hojnacki, M., Kimball, D. C., and Leech, B. L. (2009). *Lobbying and policy change: Who wins, who loses, and why*. Chicago: University of Chicago Press.

Binder, S. A. (1999). The dynamics of legislative gridlock, 1947–1996. *American Political Science Review*, *93*, 519–533.

Bonilla-Silva, E. (2017). *Racism without racists: Color-blind racism and racial inequality in contemporary America* (5th ed.). Lanhan, MD: Rowman and Littlefield Publishers, Inc.

Campbell, A., Converse, P. E., Miller, W. E., and Stokes, D. E. (1960). *The American voter*. New York: Wiley.

Carmines, E. G., and Stimson, J. A. (1989). *Issue evolution: Race and the transformation of American politics*. Princeton, NJ: Princeton University Press.

Conference, L. (2018). *Trump administration civil and human rights rollbacks*. https://civilrights.org/trump-rollbacks/.

Converse, P. E. (1964). The nature of belief systems in mass publics. In D. E. Apter (ed.), *Ideology and discontent*. Ann Arbor: University of Michigan Press.

Dancey, L. and Sheagley, G. (2011). Heuristics behaving badly: Party cues and voter knowledge. *American Journal of Political Science*, *57*, 312–325.

DeSante, C. and Smith, C.W. (2020). Fear, institutionalized racism and empathy: The underlying dimensions of whites' racial attitudes. *PS Political Science and Politics*, *53*(4), 639–645.

Egan, P. J., Persily, N., and Wallsten, K. (2008). Gay rights. In N. Persily, J. Citrin and P. Egan (eds.), *Public opinion and constitutional controversy*. New York: Oxford University Press.

Erikson, R. S., MacKuen, M. B., and Stimson, J. A. (2002). *The macro polity*. New York: Cambridge University Press.

Firebaugh, G. (1989). Methods for estimating cohort replacement effects. *Sociological Methodology*, *19*, 243–262.

Firebaugh, G. (1990). Replacement effects, cohort and otherwise: Response to Rodgers. *Sociological Methodology*, *20*, 439–446.

Firebaugh, G. (1992). Where does social change come from? Estimating the relative contributions of individual change and population turnover. *Population Research and Policy Review*, *11*, 1–20.

Glenn, N. (1976). Cohort analysts' futile quest: Statistical attempts to separate age, period and cohort effects. *American Sociological Review*, *41*(5), 900–904.

Glenn, N. (2005). Cohort analysis. *Series on Quantitative Applications in the Social Sciences*. Sage: Thousand Oaks, CA.

Hooghe, M. and Dassonneville, R. (2018). Explaining the Trump vote: The effect of racist resentment and anti-immigrant sentiments. *PS: Political Science and Politics*, *51*, 528–534.

Kellstedt, P. M. (2003). *The mass media and the dynamics of American racial attitudes*. New York: Cambridge University Press.

Kinder, D. R. and Kalmoe, N. P. (2017). *Neither liberal nor conservative: Ideological innocence in the American public*. Chicago: University of Chicago Press.

Kuklinski, J. H., Quirk, P. J., Jerit, J., Schweider, D., and Rich, R. F. (2000). Misinformation and the currency of democratic citizenship. *Journal of Politics*, *62*(3), 790–816.

Le, L. and Citrin, J. (2008). Affirmative action. In N. Persily, J. Citrin and P. Egan (eds.), *Public opinion and constitutional controversy*. New York: Oxford University Press.

Leonhardt, D. and Philbrick, I. P. (2018). Donald Trump's racism: The definitive list, updated. *The New York Times*, January 15. www.nytimes .com/interactive/2018/01/15/opinion/leonhardt-trump-racist.html.

Mayeri, S., Brown, R., Persily, N., and Kim, S. (2008). Gender equality. In N. Persily, J. Citrin, and P. Egan (eds.), *Public opinion and constitutional controversy*. New York: Oxford University Press.

Merrill, S. I., Grofman, B., and Brunell, T. L. (2008). Cycles in American national electoral politics, 1854–2006: Statistical evidence and an explanatory model. *American Political Science Review*, *102*, 1–17.

Popkin, S. L. (1991). *The reasoning voter: Communication and persuasion in presidential campaigns*. Chicago: University of Chicago Press.

Sapiro, V. and Conover, P. J. (2001). Gender equality in the public mind. *Women and Politics*, *22*, 1–36.

Schuman, H., Steeh, C., and Bobo, L. (1985). *Racial attitudes in America: Trends and interpretations*. Cambridge, MA: Harvard University Press.

Sniderman, P. M., and Carmines, E. G. (1997). *Reaching beyond race*. Cambridge, MA: Harvard University Press.

Soroka, S. and Wlezien, C. (2010). *Degrees of democracy: Politics, public opinion, and policy*. New York: Cambridge University Press.

Stimson, J. A. (1991). *Public opinion in America: Moods, cycles, and swings*. Boulder, CO: Westview Press.

Stimson, J. A. (1999). *Public opinion in America: Moods, cycles, and swings* (2nd ed.). Boulder, CO: Westview Press.

Stimson, J. A. (2004). *Tides of consent: How public opinion shapes American politics*. New York: Cambridge University Press.

Stimson, J. A. (2018). The dyad ratios algorithm for estimating latent public opinion: Estimation, testing, and comparison to other approaches. *Bulletin of Methodological Sociology, 137–138*, 201–218.

Wlezien, C. (1995). The public as thermostat: Dynamics of preferences for spending. *American Journal of Political Science, 39*(4), 981–1000.

Zhou, L. (2020). Attention has faded on the more than 20 sexual misconduct allegations against Trump. *Vox*, November 3. www.vox.com/2020/11/3/21544482/Trump-sexual-misconduct-allegations

Acknowledgments

This project had its origin at the University of North Carolina at Chapel Hill. Each of the four authors owes a debt to that university and its Department of Political Science. The National Science Foundation funded the initial phases of our research program, which produced the data series on which this Element is based. We are grateful to the Roper Center of Cornell University, which provided almost all of the public opinion data. And we are particularly grateful to Peter Enns, its director, for faultless cooperation in our efforts.

Chris Wlezien and Stuart Soroka have been friends and critics in about equal measure. Our intellectual debt to them will be obvious to any reader. We thank Bryan Jones and the Comparative Agendas team at the University of Texas at Austin.

Author Atkinson thanks colleagues in the Department of Political Science and Public Administration at the University of North Carolina, Charlotte for serving as sounding boards and for making it a pleasure to come to work. She also thanks her family for their support throughout the many years it took to complete this project.

Author Coggins thanks her co-authors for their decades-long faith in this project, Colorado College for its unyielding support of her research, her colleagues in the Political Science Department, especially Dana Wolfe, and of course, the indefatigable Jeff Kasal.

Cambridge Elements $\equiv$

American Politics

Frances E. Lee

Princeton University

Frances E. Lee is Professor of Politics at the Woodrow Wilson School of Princeton University. She is author of *Insecure Majorities: Congress and the Perpetual Campaign (2016), Beyond Ideology: Politics, Principles and Partisanship in the U.S. Senate* (2009), and coauthor of *Sizing Up the Senate: The Unequal Consequences of Equal Representation* (1999).

About the Series

The Cambridge Elements Series in *American Politics* publishes authoritative contributions on American politics. Emphasizing works that address big, topical questions within the American political landscape, the series is open to all branches of the subfield and actively welcomes works that bridge subject domains. It publishes both original new research on topics likely to be of interest to a broad audience and state-of-the-art synthesis and reconsideration pieces that address salient questions and incorporate new data and cases to inform arguments.

Cambridge Elements ≡

American Politics

Elements in the Series

A full series listing is available at:
www.cambridge.org/core/series/elements-in-american-politics

CPSIA information can be obtained
at www.ICGtesting.com
Printed in the USA
BVHW040526041121
620641BV00029B/572